The Life and Works of

JESUS

in Sequence

Conversations: Part 1

Cox Alviso

PARTRIDGE

To order additional copies of this book, contact
Toll Free +65 3165 7531 (Singapore)
Toll Free +60 3 3099 4412 (Malaysia)
orders.singapore@partridgepublishing.com

www.partridgepublishing.com/singapore

to my parents
to my siblings
to my children
to my Charissa

CONTENTS

PREFACE

This is to help my friends and loved ones start reading the Bible. You can choose to start from Genesis and weave through the astounding closure in the book of Revelations. *Or* you can start with the heart of the book. That heart is Jesus and His love for us. I hope this book will help you see that one narrative that spans the four gospels and perhaps know more about the Main Character, His struggles, His feats, the intensity of His love, and His mission. Besides, the four gospels are our best bet to knowing the Invisible (Who-Chose-to-be-Visible) God. If we can't see God in a focused cluster of books like the gospels, imagine how harder it is to find Him in the rest of the Bible.

The alleged contradictions to the four gospels sow confusion and doubt which is sad because they aren't contradictory. We find contradictions when we don't know why a piece of a jigsaw puzzle doesn't fit. We have not seen the whole picture which is why a piece looks the same as the other one. It frustrates us more because we can't tell which side goes up or down. Imagine that four-piece toy where each piece makes sense by itself but makes a bigger toy when put together. This is my attempt to put together this difficult puzzle into one toy, one puzzle that only makes sense when put together. The goal is, of course, to allow the confused reader to finally trust that Lover whose only motivation is to give us the best life the way He intended us to live and perceive.

Of course, the events captured in the gospels didn't happen in a vacuum. To put them together demand other pieces outside the essential parts that were locked in the record. To see how these stories fit in history, we need to look into whatever piece of history we could get our hands on. I had to read relevant parts of Josephus' works to find out events that surrounded the life of Herod. I had to decipher legends that surrounded the three kings. I had to look into political movements from Herod, to Quirinius, the fasts and festivals of the Jews, the ancient Roman calendar, the Jewish calendar, the Gregorian calendar, some Greek and Hebrew words and expressions, and a few notes from Saint Augustine's "Harmony of the Gospels". All this googling does not make me an expert nor a self-made scholar. What I do know is I tried to creatively put together the four gospels to one narrative with a lot of conjectures that one might say is "educated" or at the very least "opinionated" - whatever that means.

In my naiveté, I thought I am the first person to embark on this project. By the time I finished the first draft, I realised that a number of saints have attempted and succeeded. The Church has likewise recognised a number of attempts. Saint Augustine is one of my sources in straightening out a number of difficulties. His work, "Harmony of the Gospels" provided me with the lens to see how and why some accounts vary in detail. I did not get hold of the *Diatessaron* which, according to some sources, reconciled the four gospels in narrative form. Still, Saint Augustine's apologetic approach helped me decide to take notes as I was putting together this body of work. I might publish those notes in later editions of this book.

One of the difficulties I encountered after completing the 11th draft, is the problem of copyright. Apparently, I cannot directly quote from the Bible version I have. If I do, this book cannot quote more than 200 verses! I considered quoting from the many English translations in the market but even then, the syntax and differences in grammatical construction and language is too herculean of a task for a lay person like me. In the end, I had to resort to a lot of paraphrasing and whimsical rendition of many lines in street lingo or the lingo I see and hear from pop culture.

It is in this haphazard attempt to do my own "translation" work that dragged the completion of the first book (this is the first of three books). It is now seven years (2015-2022) since I started this work and I hope the reader can find, at the very least, amusement in my attempt to assemble the four gospels into one chronological narrative.

I initially wished to adopt Saint Augustine's title but realised this book is not a repeat of his work. I later decided to call it the "Markan Prerogative" because I followed Mark's general sequence which closely matches John's order. But it's an obscure title so, I considered the title, "Conjectures" because I inserted a number of conversations in the text that are not found in the Greek text. I could insert more, but I stopped at bridging a number of difficulties in the texts like Elizabeth's conversation with Mary and the reason why a number of lectures of Jesus shift from subtopic to subtopic. In the end, I took my wife's advice to pick a title that summarises the essence of what I tried to do. It is a proposed assembly of the life and works of Jesus in chronological order. So here we are. Towards the end, Conjectures became the subtitle but it is self-deprecating so I changed it to "Conversations" which is now the overarching title of the three-book series.

Last, I might not live forever, so I decided to publish whatever has been completed at this junction of my life. But I did not stop in the middle of an odd part in the life of Jesus. That would make this book feel oddly disjointed to the next book. Thank God, I finished the last event before the Holy Week (2020, I think). The Holy Week, which includes Christ's passion, is a huge chunk of this work and starts in the last third of this three-part book. If you enjoy what I accomplished in this part of the life of Jesus, you can look forward to the next book, which spans 16 months leading to the Holy Week.

To close, I hope this book will get you to embark on a life-long desire to read from God's book and learn more from Him. I can't possibly walk with you all your life, but if you read this book and found that you have personally found an open palm extended to help you, then I would find peace in knowing that God blessed this work He tasked me to accomplish.

May His Name be blessed
May His love be known
May His trust be ever established
in your heart

INTRODUCTION

This book is aimed to offer a chronological account of the life and works of Jesus based on the gospel. If you are a person who would like to start reading the Bible, this is one of the many ways to start. Read this book and know the general sequence of events from John's creation of the world, to Matthew's and Luke's recap of many fathers "begot-ing" children, to the coming of the herald and then, of course, the heart of the gospels, the Bible, and many Christians who have fallen in love: Jesus.

On Overlapping Events and Seeming Duplicates

Having no time to study what properly trained scholars learned, I am forced to resign and humbly accept that this body of work *is not* and *will never be* a proper translation. Besides, that was not my intention. Even so, I tried to make sure and capture the underlying message when putting together seemingly dissimilar accounts of events from four different writers. This is when Saint Augustine's work, "The Harmony of Gospels" became very helpful.

If one writer adds a detail that is not in the record of others, it could possibly mean that he has a reliable witness that confirms the unique information. If one writer puts a sequence ahead of another, it could possibly mean that the event happened more than once except that the second account had a different audience which needed a different approach to explain the same point in a different manner. It is for this reason that I have come to see the truth as a diamond. It has many facets that shimmer light in different sizes and colour and yet still manage to be that one same truth.

If God, allows it and grants me a longer life and sufficient resources, I might be able to publish another edition with my footnotes and reflections to various parts of His life and teachings. But first, I must complete this 3-part series.

The Sequence: Mark – John – Matthew – Luke

One of the many difficulties in assembling this is the question of which gospel writer's sequence to follow. I had to learn from a number of online sources to figure out the many overarching themes and literary tools they employed in assembling their accounts. For example, Matthew's account put together a number of lessons and parables in the Sermon on the Mount to emphasise how Jesus is the new law-giver (Moses). Matthew did this because he is presenting his case about Jesus' deeds thematically. This explains why Luke's retelling of most parables are set in different events. This means Luke recorded Jesus' deeds in a generally chronological fashion, but lumped the smaller sub stories together. This is how I noticed that Jesus' disposition on his last few months is stressed. He was on the edge and ready to bite a hater's head off because He has little time for nonsense. Jesus is about to go and people still don't get it. A very human attribute that didn't sin because He discharged His duties with grace.

As a whole, I followed the opinion of some scholars to adopt the Markan prerogative (Mark's general sequence), even though Tim Gray, one of my primary sources on this topic, suggests Matthew as the gospel writer who wrote before Mark did. Mark's chronology fits perfectly well with John's with minimal variations to Matthew's. Luke's patch to many holes in the synoptics fit where Mark's sequence logically allows. This is not a popular view because even the Church Fathers are quoted saying that Mark cared little about the order of his narrative.

To aid the reader, I have kept the verses listed at the beginning of each event so you yourself can check if you agree to the sequence I have conjectured in this book.

Location Stamp: Distance as Clue

One of my clues in determining which event came first is the geographical distance the succeeding event is from the previous. Studying the distance from event to event allowed me to investigate what manner of travel and routes they would have to take to make it happen. Oftentimes ancient travel times and modes of transportation limit the speed and distance it would take to make an event possibly happen next to another event. One example is the distance of Bethany to Jerusalem and Bethlehem to Jerusalem. Their distances to each other spelled out a sense of urgency to the events in each story, like the speed that the Magi needed to evacuate so Herod's forces in Jerusalem cannot catch them in three hours' time. Or the proximity of Bethany from Jerusalem that implied the amount of secrecy and discreteness that the huge entourage of Jesus needed to do to heal Lazarus (or camp before Holy Week) without drawing the attention of Jerusalem's assassins.

Time Stamps: Dates, History, Feasts, Fasts, Customs, Indicative Events, and Seasons

I also had to look into historical events and deep-dive into the lives of some historic figures to determine the dates I am logging in each event. Herod's is the most difficult. A number of key events in the lifetime of Jesus are tagged to Herod's activities. For example, the Church changed the calendar of the world to set the intended day of the week for an important Church celebration. Doing so revealed a mind-blowing correlation to Zechariah's service in the temple, Christmas Day, January 1, AD 1, and the date of Herod's death. When later archaeological evidences no longer support the dates we follow now, I had to resort to the resulting dates of the birth of Jesus, which is somewhere between 4 BC and AD 2. These dates are all tagged to Herod's death and correlates to where Jesus is when John (Johannes) the Baptist is executed.

Conjectures: Conversations

Last, a number of difficulties in between events and conversations were filled with my conjectures on what could have happened that resulted to each account and turn of event. Limited to the mode of publishing that I have, you will not see which parts of the text is conjecture and which part is not. I had one version where everything that wasn't in the gospels were written in grey, where the words of Jesus are all in red and God's words highlighted. There is even one that indicates which book, chapter, and verse is referred to in each sentence. That version was very hard to read.

The resulting method of bridging events resulted to the script format that the reader may or may not like. Initial feedback I received include the ease of keeping track of who is speaking. As the author, it eliminated the many times I have to write "he said," "he replied," and "she responded." This book would have been 20% bigger if I had kept that format. This method forced me to creatively write down the result of my life's worth of homily notes, daily bread musings, diary entries, and focused googling into a narrative conversation between unnamed characters to explain the motivation of the main characters, customs, and even flow of events. The result

xvi

is a full text expansion of a number of one-liners in the gospel like John's jump in Elizabeth's womb, the journey of three kings, the lively conversation of the apostles on who is greatest, and more.

Names

Most of the names I used in this book are the names used in the Gospels. A number of them are discovered from googling the character's name from the Church and other oral tradition. The names of characters like Photina, Longinus, Berenice, and others are found in many of the writings and commentaries that referred to them. While a number of said names were not confirmed by the Church, it made my job easier to use what is known, regardless of the reliability of the source.

The rest of the names that aren't found in Scripture, Oral Tradition, Church records, and Christian tradition are all conjectures. I had to come up with names, or else, it would be hard to track who said what. Following one of the rules in writing, I conserved the number of characters and limited them. As much as I admire Robert Jordan, I could not keep track of a huge number of names and keep them within character for the whole book. Surely there is more than a handful of individuals who interacted with Jesus, but the number of talking characters I named in this book is sufficient to communicate the thoughts or statements of the crowd as hinted by the Gospel writers or as supported by the pop culture of ancient times.

To the learned reader who knows Greek, Hebrew, or both, the names I conjured are often tongue in cheek. They come out as hilarious since these aren't real names but actual Greek and Hebrew words that echo the statements or disposition they had when they delivered their lines. But not all Hebrew- and Greek-sounding names are dictionary words, some really are ancient names from the culture or nation that they hailed from. Characters like the king of Armenia and the ruling king of Persia when Jesus was born are historical personalities. Their statements, however, are all made up to support the narrative written in the Gospels.

Hopes

I hope that my oddest translations will invite you to dig deep into the life of Jesus and fall in love to Him. It is my goal to give you this book as a baby walker so you can pursue a life guided by Christ through the Bible because I have come to enjoy this challenge-ridden life by walking with Him.

Chapter 1

The Gospel's Opening Texts

The Good News
about Jesus Christ,
the Son of God,
started this way . . .

~ Mark (1:1)

Luke's Preface 2
(Lk 1:1–4)

Many people wrote about the events that fulfilled the prophecies among us. These writers used eyewitness reports circulating among us from the early disciples. I too carefully investigated everything from the beginning, so I decided to write an account for you so you can be certain of the truth you were taught.

John's Introduction 3
(Jn 1:1–18)

Jesus existed in the beginning.
Jesus was with God, and
Jesus was God.

Jesus was with God in the beginning.
Everything was created through Jesus,
and nothing was created except through Jesus.

In Jesus was life,
and His life was the light of people.
Jesus' life shines through the darkness,
and darkness can't extinguish that Life.

God sent Johannes the Baptist,
to tell everyone who Jesus is
so that everyone can believe.

Johannes was simply a witness to Jesus.
Jesus is the True Light that gives light to everyone.
Jesus is coming!

"This is the One I was talking about when I said,
'The One who comes after me is greater,
because He existed before I did.'"

~ Johannes the Baptist

Jesus entered the world He created,
but the world didn't recognise Him.
He came to His own people, but even they rejected Him.
To everyone else who receive Him and believe in His Name,
He gave the right to become children of God.

Jesus became human and made His home among us. He was full of unfailing love and faithfulness. And we, apostles and other witnesses, have seen His glory, the glory of the Father's one and only Son.

No one has ever seen God. But Jesus, the begotten God in the Father's bosom, revealed Him.

Ancestors of Jesus   4
(Mt 1:1–17; Lk 3:23–38)

John highlighted how Jesus has always been God while Matthew and Luke highlighted how completely human He is. They quoted the parts of the record that shows how Jesus is the One Chosen by God, a.k.a., Messiah. These connections prove how He fits some of these prophecies: that Jesus is the heir to David's throne, the king from the line of Judah, the fulfilment of the promise to Abraham, the seed of Adam and Eve who will crush the serpent, and ultimately, the Son of God.

Matthew's record listed key people downward from Abraham to David, to the Babylonian exile, and to the Messiah. Whereas Luke tracked the lineage of Jesus all the way back to God.

Chapter 2

Birth and Childhood

GREGORIAN: 6 BC HEBREW: 3755-3756		5 BC 3756 - 3757		4 BC 3757 - 3758	
JANUARY SHEBET	JULY AV	JANUARY SHEBET	JULY TAMMUZ	13 - JESUS 1 JANUARY 2 TEBET	JULY AV
FEBRUARY ADAR	AUGUST ELUL	FEBRUARY ADAR I	AUGUST AV	14 - DEDICATION 2 FEBRUARY 5 SHEBET	AUGUST ELUL
MARCH NISAN	5 - HERALD DAY OF ATONEMENT YOM KIPPUR 22 SEPTEMBER 10 TISHRI	6 - ANNOUNCEMENT 22 MARCH 13 ADAR II	SEPTEMBER ELUL	19 - NAZARETH MARCH ADAR	SEPTEMBER TISHRI
APRIL IYAR	OCTOBER HESHVAN	7 - VISIT 7 APRIL 29 ADAR II	OCTOBER TISHRI	APRIL IYAR	OCTOBER HESHVAN
MAY SIVAN	NOVEMBER KISLEV	MAY IYAR	NOVEMBER HESHVAN	MAY SIVAN	NOVEMBER KISLEV
JUNE TAMMUZ	DECEMBER TEBET	9 - JOHANNES 24 JUNE 19 SIVAN	11 - CHRISTMAS 25 DECEMBER 25 KISLEV	JUNE TAMMUZ	DECEMBER TEBET

Calendar from 6 BC to 4 BC. The relevant event numbers are indicated with a short-form of the title (13 – JESUS is event 13 when The Baby is given the name 'Jesus' on 1 January). Equivalent Jewish year and month is likewise indicated,

Jesus is His Name

Events Leading to the Birth

Heads Up for the Herald   5
(Lk 1:5–25)

During Herod the Great's reign in Judea (40-1 BCE), there was a Jewish priest named Zechariah. He was a member of the priestly order of Abijah, while Elizabeth, his wife, was also from the priestly line of Aaron. They were very old, and they had no children, even though they were righteous in God's eyes.

Time Stamp   : Wednesday, 22 September 6 BC
                    Day of Atonement (*Yom Kippur*)
Location Stamp   : Temple, Jerusalem

Zechariah was serving God in the temple. He was a descendant of Aaron, and the line of Abijah's family was on duty. He was picked according to the custom of the priests to enter the Lord's temple and burn incense. A huge assembly prayed at the temple grounds as incense is burned inside the Sanctuary.

Zechariah was shocked when an angel of the Lord appeared next to the Altar of Incense. He was gripped in fear when the angel spoke,

Angel:

> Don't be afraid! God heard your prayer. Your wife will give birth to your son. Name him Johannes. He will give you joy and happiness. Many will celebrate his birth because he will be great in God's eyes. He must never drink wine or any strong drink.

He will be filled with the Holy Spirit
before he is born,
and he will turn many Israelites
back to God.
He will serve before God
in the spirit and power of Elijah.
He will prepare the people
for the Lord's coming
by turning the hearts
of parents to their children,
and rebels to the wisdom
of those who are righteous.

Zechariah: Am I the right person? I'm an old man, and so is my wife.

Angel: I am Gabriel! I see God myself, and I was sent to give you great news.

  But since you do not believe, you will not speak and stay quiet until this happens.

Outside, people wondered what's taking him so long. When he finally came out, he couldn't speak anymore. He was mute, but based on his gestures, they figured out that he must have seen a vision in the temple.

Time Stamp : 12:00 n.n., Sabbath, 25 September 6 BC
Location Stamp : Jerusalem
Indicative Event : Aaronic priests hand over
  their responsibilities to the next family on duty.

Time Stamp : 25 September 6 BC (Tishri 13)
Indicative Event : Zechariah departs Jerusalem after 6:00 p.m. (end of Sabbath day) and reached Hebron later that night.

When his service was over, he went home to the hills of Judea. That night, Elizabeth became pregnant. To assure a successful pregnancy, she went into seclusion for five months.

Announcement!

"Jesus, who is the true light,
is coming into the world."

~ Johannes

Annunciation   6
(Mt 1:18a; Lk 1:26–38)

Time Stamp   : 22 March 5 BC (13 Adar II), Fast of Esther
Indicative Event : First day of Elizabeth's sixth month of pregnancy

---

Mary was engaged to Joseph

~ Matthew (1:18a)

Time Stamp   : Sabbath, 25 March 5 BC (16 Adar II)
Location Stamp   : Nazareth, Palestinia

On the sixth month of Elizabeth's pregnancy, God sent His angel, Gabriel, to Mary, His virgin. She was engaged to Joseph, a descendant of King David.

Gabriel: Greetings, you who are favoured with grace!
              Of all women, you are blessed.
              The Lord is with you.

Mary: What??

Gabriel: Don't be afraid, Mary! God chose you.
              You will name your Son, Jesus,
              whom you will conceive and deliver.

He will be great. He will be called,
"the Son of the Most High."
The Lord God will give Him
the throne of His father, David.
He will rule over the house of Jacob forever
and His Kingdom will never end!

Mary: But how? I am a virgin.

Gabriel: The Holy Spirit will come to you
and God's power will overshadow you.

The Holy Infant will be called,
"Son of God."

By the way, your old cousin Elizabeth is pregnant
with a son! People say she's barren, but she's
already on her sixth month, because nothing is
impossible to God.

Mary: I am God's servant.
May everything you said come true.

Then Gabriel left.

Mary tells Joseph
(Mt 1:18b–24)

Time Stamp   : Shortly after 6:00 p.m., 25 March 5 BC
(Sabbath ends at 6:00 p.m.)

---

before they were married,
she was made pregnant by the Holy Spirit

~ Matthew (1:18b)

10

Mary told Joseph, her fiancé, what happened and that she is pregnant.

Joseph: Who else was there when the angel appeared?

Mary: Just me.

Joseph: There is no way I can confirm the truth if you're the only witness.

Mary: I know but didn't Samson's father, Manoah, believe his wife when the angel first appeared?

Joseph: I pray the angel does appear again so I can be assured.

Mary: ...

Joseph: Please let me think about this tonight. I don't know what's going on and I don't know what to do.

Mary turns to leave,

Joseph: Thank you for letting me know. I'd rather hear it from you than anyone else.

Joseph was a righteous person and did not want to make this public, so he planned to send her away secretly. Having thought about these things he slept and was visited by the Lord's angel in a dream.

Malakh: Joseph, son of David,
don't be afraid to take Mary as your wife

because the baby she conceived
in the Spirit is Holy.

She will deliver a Son.
Name Him Jesus
because He will save His people
from their sins.

All this is happening to fulfil God's message
through Isaiah, His prophet:

"LOOK! THE VIRGIN WILL CONCEIVE, AND GIVE BIRTH TO A SON. THEY WILL CALL HIM IMMANUEL, WHICH MEANS 'GOD IS WITH US.'"

~ God Almighty

Time Stamp   : Sunday, 6:00 a.m., 26 March 5 BC

When Joseph woke up, he obeyed the command from God's messenger and prepared for the wedding celebration.

Time Stamp   : Tuesday, 28 March 5 BC
Indicative Event   : Joseph & Mary got married on the 3rd day of the week, the preferred day to get married

Joseph and Mary got married but he never touched her.

Time Stamp   : Tuesday, 29 March to 3 April 5 BC
Indicative Event   : Week-long wedding celebration
according to custom

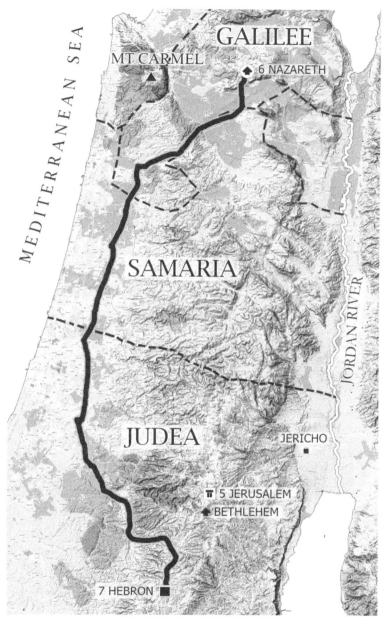

Mary and Joseph's route
from Nazareth to the Hills of Judea to visit Elizabeth

"The king rose to meet her, and bowed down to her;
then he sat on his throne,
and had a throne brought for the king's mother"

1 Kings 2:19b-c, NRSV

Queen's Visit   7
(Lk 1:39–45)

Time Stamp   : Friday, 7 April 5 BC (29 Adar II)
Location Stamp   : Zechariah's home, somewhere in Hebron, Judea

After their wedding, Mary hurried to one of the towns in the hills of Judea. She entered Zechariah's house and saw Elizabeth undeniably pregnant.

Mary:	Greetings my dear Elizabeth! What have you been eating lately?

At the sound of Mary's greeting, Elizabeth's child moved, and she was filled with the Holy Spirit. Off-balanced, Mary caught Elizabeth as she winced at her discomfort.

Elizabeth:	Look at what God did! He took away my disgrace.

They laughed as Elizabeth told Mary what happened to Zechariah while serving at the temple six months ago.

Mary:	I was there on the Day of Atonement! Well, everyone is, but everyone did think it weird that the presiding priest was taking a long time to get out. You can hear the crowd sigh with relief when Zechariah walked out but even then, no one

14

heard the blessing reach to the back of the crowd. When the crowd started dissipating, everyone assumed that the Shema has been given.

Elizabeth: Thank God, my husband can write. He came home with a copy of his report to the chief priests. I could not believe he saw an angel, but how else can we explain why he is mute?

Mary: He saw an angel?!

Elizabeth: Yes, Gabriel was the name, he said. It is the same angel that told us I will conceive, and well, look at me now!

Mary: Did you say Gabriel? That was the same angel that appeared to me! It was the same angel that told me that you are pregnant.

Elizabeth: Really?! What else did God's angel say?

Mary then told her the message and said that she carries the Son of God in her womb. Elizabeth was mind-blown as the churning baby in her womb now made sense.

Elizabeth: God blessed you over all women!
Your Child is blessed.
Who am I to be visited
by my King's mother?
No wonder my baby jumped for joy
when I heard your greeting.
You are blessed for believing
that the Lord would do what He said.

Elizabeth broke down thinking about Zechariah's condition. Again, Mary rushed to comfort her.

Song Sequence #1   8
(Lk 1:46–56)

Mary:	My soul declares the Lord's greatness.
	My spirit celebrates in God, my Saviour!
	Look, He noticed me
	even though I'm only His servant.
	From now on,
	all generations will call me blessed
	because the Almighty, whose Name is Holy,
	has done great things for me.

He is merciful to those who fear Him
from generation to generation.
He display His powerful arm.
He scattered people
with pride in their heart.
He dethrones leaders
and appoints the humble.

He loads the hungry with good things
and exiles rich people empty-handed.
He helps His servant Israel
and remembers to be merciful
just as He said to our ancestors,
Abraham and His descendants forever.

Time Stamp   : 12 April 5 BC (5 Nisan)
Indicative Event : The whole family travels to Jerusalem
                    to celebrate Passover

Time Stamp   : 14-20 April 5 BC
Location Stamp   : Jerusalem, Palestinia
Indicative Event : The whole family arrives in Jerusalem and observes the week-long cleansing ritual/ceremony

Time Stamp   : 21-28 April 5 BC
Location Stamp   : Jerusalem, Palestinia
Indicative Event : Passover & Feast of Unleavened Bread

Time Stamp   : 29 April 5 BC
Indicative Event : Whole family heads back to Zechariah's home

Mary decided to stay with Elizabeth for about three months.

Herald, Hot and Fresh!   9
(Lk 1:57–66)

Time Stamp   : Saturday, 24 June 5 BC
Location Stamp   : Zechariah's home, Hebron

In the ninth month of Elizabeth's pregnancy, she gave birth to a son. As soon as her neighbours and relatives heard this, they declared how great the Lord is and celebrated God's mercy to her.

Time Stamp   : Saturday, 1 July 5 BC

On the eighth day, the child was scheduled for circumcision in accordance with the law.

Nagash: Alright now, we'll give him
              his father's name, Zechariah.

Elizabeth: No! Name him Johannes!

Nagash: What?! No one in your family has that name.

So, they asked Zechariah what to name him by some sort of sign language. He pointed to a writing tablet, and to everyone's surprise, he wrote, "His name is Johannes."

"God sent a man:
Johannes the Baptist"

~ John

Zechariah was instantly healed. The moment he realised it, he blessed God.

Zechariah's Prophecy   10
(Lk 1:67–79)

Filled with the Holy Spirit, he prophesied.

Zechariah: Happy is the Lord, God of Israel!
Because He visited His people
and redeemed them.

As He said long ago,
through the holy mouth of His prophets,
He raised for us a Saviour
in the house of His servant, David.
Now we will be saved
from our enemies
and everyone who hates us.

He raised for us a Saviour
to give mercy to our ancestors,
and remember His sacred covenant,
the promise He gave
our father Abraham

18

He raised for us a Saviour,
to free us from fear of our enemies
so we can serve Him with dedication
and righteousness all our life.

You, my son, will be called
prophet of the Most High
because you will prepare
the way of the King.
You will tell God's people
how to find salvation
in the forgiveness of their sins.

Through God's deep compassion,
we'll see heaven's Sunrise visit us
to bring light to those in darkness,
to bring light to those
who sit in the shadows of death,
and to guide us to the way of peace.

While everyone in the hills of Judea talked about his prophecy, everyone in the neighbourhood was afraid. Those who heard the news kept it in their hearts.

Sim: What will Johannes be?
God's hand is with him.

Time Stamp : Sunday, 2 July 5 BC

After all these events, Mary and Joseph went back
to their home in Nazareth.

Enter the King!

God is... Born? 11

(Lk 2:1a,2–7; Mt 1:25a)

These events happened during the reign of Emperor Caesar Augustus.

Time Stamp   : 21 December 5 BC
Location Stamp   : Nazareth, Palestinia
Indicative Event : Sagrada Familia left Nazareth

Joseph went from Nazareth, Galilee to Bethlehem, Judea, which is King David's hometown, because he was a descendant of David. Mary, who is in her ninth month of pregnancy, came with him.

Time Stamp   : before 6:00 p.m., 24 December 5 BC
Location Stamp   : Bethlehem, Palestinia
Indicative Event : Sagrada Familia arrives in Bethlehem

When they reached Bethlehem, they looked for a place to stay.

Joseph: You must be the innkeeper. Can you give us a room? We're here for the celebration and my wife needs a good cot to rest.

Bet: Yikes, you will have a problem getting a room. Everyone is here in Jerusalem for Hanukkah.

Joseph: Oh, right. Tomorrow is Hanukkah.

Bet: The city's inns are packed. That's why a lot of them look for accommodations around the city. The size of the annual pilgrims has increased in the last few years.

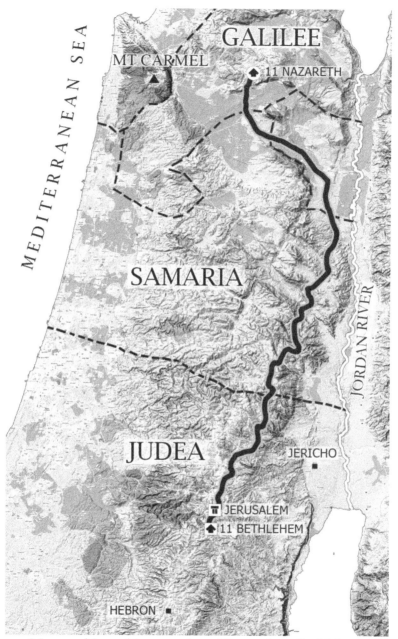

Mary and Joseph's route from Nazareth to Bethlehem

Joseph: Do you have a small room at least?

Bet: I'm sorry, my rooms are all taken and the last group I referred to my neighbour couldn't be accommodated either. I heard some pilgrims already headed out to Bethany and Emmaus for a place to stay. It is a bit late. You better hurry out.

Joseph: I understand. Thank you.

Joseph and Mary tried a few more inns but it seems the innkeeper's forecast is accurate.

Joseph: So how? It's late. We still have some food left. We could eat on the road. Maybe we can still reach the nearest town if we ride a bit faster.

Mary: I guess I can still manage another kilometre or two. Bethany is too close to Jerusalem. It should be filled by now.

Joseph: Emmaus is much further. How about Zechariah's place at Hebron?

Mary: Herodium is closer. I think I can still handle the cramps.

Not long after they left the gates of Bethlehem, Mary went into labour.

Joseph: Hold on, we're in the middle of nowhere. I better find shelter.

Mary: How about that tower?

Joseph:	A flock tower? I'm not sure if we're allowed there.
Mary:	Ow! Ow! Ow! If there are shepherds nearby then at least we have someone who can help us. Hurry!
Joseph:	Look! There's a boy. Maybe he can help us.
Mary:	Beg for help! Ooooh! Go! Go! Go!
Joseph:	Young man, can you let us inside your tower? My wife is going into labour. We can't give birth on the road.
Roi:	I don't think you are allowed to do that. The delivery will desecrate the room.
Joseph:	Please, I beg you.
Mary:	Aaaah!
Roi:	I don't know what to do!
Joseph:	Please? Look! There's a shed. Can you at least get us a few things we need?
Mary:	Hurry! Aaagh!
Roi:	That old cave? There are bulls there with other . . .
Joseph:	*eyes narrowing*
Roi:	All right, go! I think I have other things you might need. I think we have an old manger for the baby in the tower too. I'll get it for you.

Birth and Childhood

Joseph hurried and took Mary in. After a few more hours of labour, she delivered The Son.

Time Stamp   :   25 December 5 BC
Location Stamp   :   Still in Bethlehem, Palestinia

He came into the world He created

He came to His people

God became human and lived among us.
His love and faithfulness are reliable.
We saw His glory,
the glory of the Father's one and only Son.

~ John

She wrapped her firstborn Son in cloth strips then laid Him in a manger. Joseph never made love with her even after she delivered The Son.

In other news . . .

Time Stamp   :   Evening between 24 & 25 December 5 BC
Location Stamp   :   Keralaputra, Tamilakam

Hitansh: Swami, Aabha saw something of interest in the night sky.

Gizbar: What is it?

Hitansh: She said, this could be the star Swami Belatashasaar talked about.

Looks at the night sky. Wide eyed.

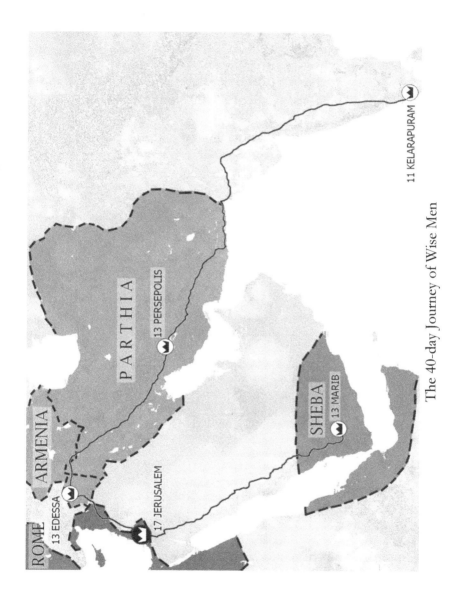

The 40-day Journey of Wise Men

Gizbar:	Prepare for a long travel. Bring some cash, and don't forget to bring the horn.
Hitansh:	Travel to where, my Swami?
Gizbar:	The star is moving west and fast. Pack for two weeks' worth of travel. Nope, make it one month.
Hitansh:	You will be travelling to dangerous lands!
Gizbar:	I know. Order Patr to get his men ready. We'll leave tomorrow.

Song Sequence #2   12
(Lk 2:8–20)

Time Stamp   : Same evening between 24 and 25 December 5 BC
Location Stamp : Shepherds' fields around Bethlehem

That same night, shepherds were guarding their flocks in fields nearby.

Dave:	It's gonna be a busy day tomorrow morning.
Yaqub:	You said it. By now, Jerusalem is probably packed with a lot of people.
Dave:	A lot of our sheep is going to be sacrificed later.
Yaqub:	I have asked my nephew to pick a new batch to be sent tomorrow to the temple.
Dave:	I already sent about 300 from my flock yesterday.

Yaqub: What do you think? We will be celebrating Hanukkah, the dedication of the temple, later.

Dave: It's hard to celebrate when the ark has not been found and there's no sign of liberation from these gentiles!

Yaqub: Yeah, we've been waiting forever. When will our liberator come?

Thaddai: Are you guys talking about the Messiah?

Dave: Yep. We were talking about Hanukkah and our busy day tomorrow.

Thaddai: And the next few days!!

Yaqub: How was your trip to Jerusalem earlier? Did the guards take another one of your sheep?

Thaddai: Shameless gentile pigs! *spits*

Yaqub: Yeah! If the Messiah comes tomorrow, I'll join His army and circumcise those dicks!

Dave: Hahaha! As if your slingshot can take them down. Those helmets sure can handle our rocks.

Yaqub: Doesn't matter. If David can take down a giant, surely we can do it too. If only we have the King to save us.

Dave: Well, you'll be the first to know. I heard He will come from Bethlehem. We can't be the last people to know. Haha!

Yaqub:	What if you are the Messiah? Didn't Micah say that He will come from the flock tower?
Dave:	Hahaha. I may be from the tribe of Judah, but I wasn't born from the royal line of David.
Thaddai:	Yeah, it also said somewhere that we won't know where He'll come from.
Dave:	Besides, this is only one of many towers around the city.
Yaqub:	Sigh! When will deliverance come?

All of a sudden, an angel of the Lord appeared and God's glory surrounded them. The shepherds were freaked out. Big time!

Shenimalak: Calm down!
I bring good news
that'll make all people celebrate.

Today, The Saviour is born for you.
Yes, the Lord, the Chosen One,
is born today in David's city!
You will recognise Him in a manger
as a baby wrapped in cloth strips.

Out of nowhere, the angel was accompanied by the vast armies of heaven praising God.

Armies of Heaven:

Glory to God in the highest heavens!
and peace to people on earth
who please Him.

After the angels left, the shepherds gathered.

Ed: Did you guys see that?

Dave: How can you not? Everywhere I look in the night sky, it's all angels, angels, angels!

Sahed: They said the Chosen One is here!
The Messiah is here!

Chaphar: Come! Let's go to Bethlehem!
That is David's city, right?

Ed: Is it? Isn't Jerusalem the city of David?

Dave: It's Bethlehem. We don't need to go very far. It can only be Bethlehem.

Thaddai: I agree, we can't go to Jerusalem tonight. No one will look after the flock.

Yaqub: Let's go! I want to see what this announcement is about, up close!

Ed: Where do we begin? The town is full of people! It could be any manger!

Chaphar: Let's start with the ones in our towers. A few of us will have to stay behind.

Thaddai: I'll stay behind.
But I'll blow the horn if I need help.

Tur: Hey guys! You saw that too?

Yaqub:	Yes, we'll search the towers for a baby in swaddling first, before we search the city.
Dave:	Someone blow the horn if you find anything. Otherwise, let's all meet back here.
Tur:	You know what? You search the towers while I get other guys to search the city.
Chaphar:	Let's go!

They ran and searched all known mangers until they found Mary and Joseph, Sure enough, The Baby lay in a manger as announced by Heaven's Armies.

Yaqub:	*gasp* It's true!! Blow the horn quick!
Chaphar:	What is our signal? We didn't decide earlier Hahaha!
Yaqub:	The call for victory in war!
Chaphar:	The Hallel?
Yaqub:	How about the Hoshannah?
Chaphar:	I'll blow Hoshannah to the highest.

Shocked and happy that the Saviour they waited for over 1000 years is finally here, the shepherds told everyone what the Army of Angels said and The Baby they found. Everyone who heard their story were in awe.

Bet:	Oh no! I think I saw that couple earlier. Quick dear! Clear our room!

Tur: What do you want me to do?

Bet: When you find them, please ask them to come over. Bring the cart. The room should be ready by the time they arrive.

Mary treasured all these things and thought about them in her heart.

The shepherds left glorifying and praising God for witnessing everything they were told.

Circumcision and Naming Day   13
(Lk 2:21; Mt 1:25b)

"EVERY MALE AMONG YOU WHO IS EIGHT DAYS OLD MUST BE CIRCUMCISED. MY COVENANT IN YOUR FLESH IS TO BE AN EVERLASTING COVENANT."

~ God Almighty
(Gen 17: 12b, 13b)

Time Stamp   : 1 January 4 BC
Location Stamp   : Bethlehem, Palestinia

On the day eighth day, The Baby was circumcised. They named Him, Jesus. The name the angel said before He was conceived.

Time Stamp   : 14 January 4 BC
Location Stamp   : Persepolis, Parthian Empire

Meanwhile, somewhere in Parthia, a young man with a band of riders knocked on the door of a Persian wise man.

Hor: Welcome! My people saw you coming and have told me of your arrival. What can I do for you?

Gizbar: Greetings my dear Maharajadhirajah! We are travellers from the land of gods. I hail from Tamilakam from the land that face the great west sea. We are here to pay homage and worship the King of Kings.

Hor: Please forgive me, but I am not a king, nor am I the King of Kings. What made you think I am your Maharajadhirajah?

Gizbar: I am a leader among my people and I come here to look for the King that the wise man, Belatashaar, prophesied about 600 years ago.

Hor: Your accent is quite thick young man. Belatashaar seems familiar. Can you tell me more about him and this King? I might know who you are referring to.

Gizbar had his servant open a scroll containing a copy of Daniel's prophesies about the King as they checked and counter checked each other's record.

Hor: You are, indeed, referring to the great Belteshazzar, servant and adviser to the great emperors, a true prophet of the Living God. If you are correct, I am guessing that the new King is who you are referring to. He is Ukkāmā of the northwest end of the empire. I did not think he is the King from the prophecies unless the star you refer to points to him.

Gizbar: You can look outside right now. It stopped here a few days ago while we were chasing it. That is why we came here thinking you are the great King.

They went out and Hor was stunned at the sight of the star!

Gizbar: Oh no! Patr!

Patr: I am here, Swami.

Gizbar: Order your men to prepare to move.
           The star is on the move again.

Hor: Navid! We have great news!

Navid: My Shah, what can I do for you?

Hor: Mani Belteshazzar's prophesy is here! The star of the King is upon us, and it is on the move!

Navid: Shall I inform the other manis of the land, my Shah?

Hor: Send a bird to Bithisarea and tell him Mani Belteshazzar's star has risen. Tell him to follow the star and that we are headed to its destination.

Gizbar: Shah, my friend, I regret to cut our visit short, but we need to catch that star.

Hor: My friend, Swami, kindly wait for me. I will join you and bring gifts myself. I too wish to worship the Great King.

| Gizbar: | I will stay back for a bit, but my men need fresh supplies and we cannot allow the star to travel so far that we might have problems running after it. |

| Hor: | I completely understand. Please accept my thanks. |

| Gizbar: | Hold on, won't you get in trouble with your king? |

| Hor: | Who? Shan Phraates IV? He is weak and wedded to an enemy's spy. A slave's bridegroom can never be my king. |

Time Stamp : 22 January 4 BC
Location Stamp : Ma'rib, Sheba

| Banjaw: | Sultan, a message arrived for you. It seems urgent. |

| Bithisarea: | Please read it for me, Banjaw. |

| Banjaw: | Bithisarea, my friend, my sultan, peace be upon you and your people. Look at the sky and know that Mani Beltheshazzar's star is on its way to . . . |

| Bithisarea: | Go on, Banjaw. I'm listening. Don't stop now. |

| Banjaw: | It's the star of Negusa Nagast, my Sultan! |

| Bithisarea: | What?! Hand me that message. |

With hands shaking, Banjaw hands it to Bithisarea. He then bowed low on the ground, which cued everyone around them to bow low.

Bithisarea: What in the . . .?

Bithisarea quickly ran to the nearest window and looked up the sky, and as he realised what he was looking at, he quickly issued a flurry of instructions.

Bithisarea: Quick Banjaw. Move on the double! I'm not sure if my friend has reached the King.

Banjaw: When are you leaving?

Bithisarea: First thing tomorrow. Get our finest product. Put it in a new stone jar.

Banjaw: Stone? Lapiz Lazuli or Pink Egyptian Marble?

Bithisarea: Alabaster! We're talking about the King of Kings! And tell Defere to prepare the fastest camels. We might be behind schedule.

Time Stamp   : 29 January 4 BC
Location Stamp : Edessa, Osroene (modern day Turkey)

Abgar V: What brings you to my land?

Hor: We come to honour the King of Kings.

Abgar V: What have I done
                to deserve such honourable title?

Gizbar: The prophecy of the Great King is preceded by a star, and that star appeared a few days ago and has led us here.

Abgar V:	It seems that my court astrologers have seen this star, but it seems a bit way off. Down to the south, I think. Are you sure I am the one you seek?
Gizbar:	. . .
Hor:	Is it? Pardon us as we check.
Abgar V:	Please do.
Navid:	Magush, his majesty is correct. The star seems to stand a bit south from where we are.
Hor:	This is embarrassing, your Highness.
Abgar V:	While you are here, do you mind telling me about this King of Kings.

The two visitors told the prophecy of Daniel and the star that has appeared, also of the prophecy about this King.

Abgar V:	You have a huge contingent heading to the south. If you leave the empire's territory, you will have difficulty navigating enemy territory safely. You'd be lucky to reach the King without meeting another army.
Hor:	You speak the truth, your highness. What do you suggest?
Abgar V:	Leave most of your men and camels here and take my horses with you. You'll be able to travel faster. I'll send my ambassador too, to help you navigate away from cities where governors sit.

Hor: We do not wish to bother your people,
                your highness.

Abgar V: No please. I insist. I too would like to see the King
                myself. I hope He will recognise my gifts by the
                people I send with you.

Hor: We thank you your highness.

Gizbar: If I may, your highness, the star moves south fast.
                We'll need to leave soon.

Abgar V: I understand. We'll leave tonight.

the temple meets The Temple   14
(Lk 2:22-27, 36–37)

Time Stamp   : 2 February 4 BC
Location Stamp : Temple, Jerusalem

When Mary completed the 40-day purification period after giving
birth, the law of Moses required her to present a purification
offering. While they're at it, they took Jesus to the temple in
Jerusalem to present Him to the Lord, as written in God's law:

"All male firstborn child must be dedicated to God."

That day, the Holy Spirit led Simeon to the temple. He was a devout
and righteous man eagerly waiting for the consolation of Israel. The
Holy Spirit told him before that he will not die until he sees the
Lord's Chosen.

Anna, the daughter of Phanuel, was also there in the temple, at that
time. She is an old prophetess from the tribe of Asher who was

married for seven years. It has been 84 years since she was widowed. She practically lived in the temple. Day and night, she stayed there praying, fasting, and serving.

When they reached the Temple, they brought the required purification sacrifice in the law of the Lord which is either a pair of turtledoves or two young pigeons.

"Grant me Peace" ~ Simeon   15
(Lk 2:28–35, 38a)

Anna watched the couple approaching the temple and recognised the virgin!

Anna:	Mary? Is it really you?
Mary:	Yes, I am, Anna.
Joseph:	Greetings Anna! A lot has changed here in short time. What is that eagle?
Anna:	Herod put it there. The priests are outraged. *rolls eyes*
Mary:	Anna, look!
Anna:	What?! But, but, but, didn't you swear to dedicate your body to the temple, to the Lord?
Mary:	I did.
Anna:	Then what am I looking at?

Joseph: Should I tell her?

Anna: Joseph, my dear, didn't you know she has a promise to God?

Joseph: I know, but . . .

Mary: It's okay, Joseph...

Mary told Anna what has happened in the last few months. Anna's jaw dropped at each turn of event.

Anna: Praise God Almighty! So, if you're not here to offer the guilt offering to break your vow, what are you here for?

Mary: It has been forty days, and we're here to dedicate my firstborn to the Lord.

Anna: My dear God! Of course! Of course! Hold on, I'll call Simeon.

When Simeon heard about Jesus, he hurried to see Him. When he finally saw Jesus, he held the Child and blessed God.

Simeon:

Lord, my eyes have seen Your salvation,
the salvation You prepared for everyone to see.
He is the glory of Your people, Israel!
He is the light for the world to see.

Lord, dismiss Your servant now
in peace, like You promised me.

The father and mother of Jesus were amazed at what was said about Him. Simeon blessed them too, then he turned to Mary.

Simeon: Look, this Child
is picked to destroy many
is picked to resurrect many
and a sign picked to be opposed vehemently.

In Him, a sword will go through your soul to expose the thoughts in the heart of many people.

Anna's News   16
(Lk 2:38b–39a)

Anna praised God and told everyone who waited for Jerusalem's redemption that the Baby is finally here.

After the parents of Jesus completed the requirements of God's law, they went back to Bethlehem.

Wise Men finds Wisdom   17
(Mt 2:1-12)

Time Stamp   : 4 February 4 BC (Shebat 7)
Location Stamp   : Outside Jerusalem

Hor: I thought you'll never make it, old friend!

Bithisarea: Between you and me,
I think you are old. Haha!

Hor: Haha! Come, I'll introduce you to this fine young man from the land that faces the great western sea.

Gizbar:	Pleased to meet you, Sultan. My name is Gizbar.
Bithisarea:	Gizbar? From Kelaraputra?
Gizbar:	I'm sorry. Do I know you?
Bithisarea:	It is me! You trade with my people – the people of Sheba!
Gizbar:	Land of the most fragrant spices?
Bithisarea:	Next to your spices, yes!
Gizbar:	Holy God! What a small world!
Hor:	You know each other?
Bithisarea:	Yes, the last message I got from him is that the star he has been waiting for has finally arrived. I actually know him from his father.
Gizbar:	The gift I bring was prepared by my father who now sleeps among the stars.
Bithisarea:	I am sorry. I did not know.
Gizbar:	It is all right. I believe he will be happy to know that I brought the gift that he wanted to bring himself to the Maharajadhirajah.
Bithisarea:	The famed myrrh of Tamilakam, and . . . is that black gold?

Hor: That was from your country?

Gizbar: *bows*

Bithisarea: Come, everyone. Our star has finally rested on this great city. Let us seek first the Negusa Nagast before we continue this chat.

Hor: Do you know who we came for?

Bithisarea: I know Herod. I didn't think this Edomite is the King of Kings, but maybe one of his sons is.

Gizbar: Come. The journey has been long for me.

Location Stamp : Herod's Palace, Inside Jerusalem

Translator: Where is the King of Jews? We saw His star rise from the east and travelled far to worship Him.

Herod: I am the king of the Jews and a friend of Caesar. What can I do for you?

Translator: Your majesty, pardon the confusion. We seek a child, a new-born child. The star that rose signalled His birth. Perhaps it is your son that we seek.

Herod: All my children are full-grown men, capable to take my throne. You must be referring to one of them.

Translator: Our sincere apologies, your majesty. My masters are wise men who are certain of the signs they saw in the sky.

Herod:	Please allow me to consult my advisers. Perhaps they can interpret what you seek.

Herod received the huge contingent and had them entertained. Meanwhile, Jerusalem was abuzz with the foreigners and the question they asked. Herod summoned all the chief priests and scribes, and as soon as they were assembled, he started interrogating them.

Herod:	Where is the Messiah's birthplace?
Razili:	In Bethlehem, Judea. According to our source, the prophet Micah wrote,

"BETHLEHEM, AMONG JUDAH'S LEADING CITIES, YOU ARE NOT THE LEAST BECAUSE THE SHEPHERD WHO WILL LEAD MY PEOPLE WILL COME FROM YOU."

~ Almighty God

Herod did not know if the embassy will kill or support the King who can overthrow him and his Roman allies. So, he invited the wise men to a private meeting.

Herod:	You seem tired from your travel. You must have come from afar.
Translator:	Yes, indeed, your majesty. Some of us have come from the Far East.
Herod:	Quite far! When did you leave your people?

Translator: As soon as we saw the star rise, we immediately started packing.

Herod: When was that?

Translator: It was spotted over 40 days ago. It led us to this city.

Herod: You must have travelled fast to get here.

Translator: We did. It is the Most High King that we are talking about. We are eager to pay homage and earn His favour. Coming from this far out, we are afraid to be the last of those who worship Him. It does confuse us why you don't seem to know where He is.

Herod: I do. I do. I do. You can find Him in Bethlehem just a short camel's walk outside this city. We are still preparing our gifts to Him, see? We do not wish to be outdone by foreign kings. Hahaha!

Translator: We are grateful for this information, your majesty. With this, we must now make a move to find Him.

Herod: I see. We have been looking for Him too, and this star is not so clear on its directions. Please look more carefully on my behalf and let me know once you find Him. Here, I send you my servant, Yehudah, to guide you in your travel. Please send word as soon as you find Him. I must worship Him too!

The wise men left after the meeting.

Patr:	Swami, the star is on the move again.
Gizbar:	It is heading south.
Bithisarea:	According to my translator, Herod's servant said that city to the south is Bethlehem.
Gizbar:	Then we are in the right direction.
Hor:	We shall soon see Him. Let's go everyone.
Location Stamp :	A house in Bethlehem, Judea
Yehudah:	We are looking for a King. Perhaps you know where He is hiding?
Joseph:	?? There are no kings here. Who are these people?
Yehudah:	They are King Herod's guests. They are looking for a King. *snort*
Translator:	Greetings! My masters came here from afar. We seek the King of Kings.
Joseph:	I am a descendant of King David but I am not the one you seek. I think I know Who you are all looking for. Please come inside.

When they finally stood in the Child's audience, they bowed and worshiped Him. The wise men, their contingent, and all noble men and women who came with them opened their treasure chests and gave Him gifts.

Hor: Xšâyathiya Xšâyathiyânâm, Your Highness, kindly accept this humble gift. Truly, my God has humbled me today *breaks down*. I do not deserve to stand before the King and His Basilissa.

Joseph: Thank you, kind sir. *whispers* Mary, look! A box full of golden figs!

Mary: . . .

Bithisarea: Negusa Nagast, Almighty, kindly accept this lowly gift.

Joseph: Thank you, kind sir. This is alabaster! What fragrance is locked in this huge jar?

Bithisarea: The finest frankincense ever sold in the Kingdom of Sheba.

Joseph: . . .

Gizbar: Maharajadhirajah, Your Majesty, kindly accept this unworthy gift.

Joseph: This is one big golden horn! What is this fragrance I smell?

Gizbar: It is the finest myrrh from the Far East.

Joseph: Isn't this . . .

| Mary: | Yes, dear, these gifts are fit for the King of Kings. |

| Joseph: | This calls for a celebration! Please rest. We'll have your meals served shortly. |

The huge embassy celebrated that night, and everyone rested in their tents.

Later that night, God warned them in a dream about Herod's plot. They woke up and found out their "escort," Yehudah, is missing.

| <u>B</u>ithisarea: | Come my friends. It is not wise to travel north where Herod can chase us. |

| <u>H</u>or: | I know. But we can't travel east. That will run through the desert. We do not have enough supplies to make it through the trip. |

| <u>B</u>ithisarea: | Let us journey fast to my country to the south. From there, Gizbar can take a ship back to his country. |

| <u>N</u>avid: | Magush, there is a merchant's route through the east side of the great desert. We can take that road on our way back from Sheba to Persepolis. |

| <u>H</u>or: | Let us go then. Herod should be back by morning light. |

Save the babies   18
(Mt 2:13–14, 16–18)

Time Stamp   : 5 February 4 BC (evening between 4 & 5 February)

47

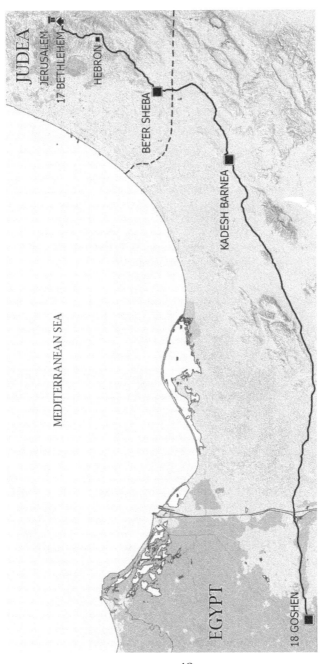

3-week Escape from Bethlehem to Egypt

God likewise, warned Joseph in a dream.

Shlishimalak: Quick! Get up! Run to Egypt and stay there with the Child and His mother until I tell you. Herod will come to kill the Child.

Joseph woke up at the fourth watch and took Jesus and His mother to Egypt.

Herod arrived in Bethlehem that morning but didn't find neither wise men nor the King's family. Furious that the wise men tricked him, he sent soldiers to round up all infant boys.

Herod: Is this all of them?

Yehudah: Yes, lord.

Herod: Do you recognise any of them?

Yehudah: None. It seems these people are hiding them.

Herod: Tell them the traitor who hides The Boy will die today if they do not tell me where He is!

Yehudah: My lord, it seems that This Boy was recently found in the temple and associated to the temple virgins and some priests.

Herod: How recent is this, "recent"?

Yehudah: Some say a few days ago, some say last year.

Herod: *fuming* Gather all infant boys around Bethlehem. Include all boys born last year.

49

Yehudah: Last year?

Herod: Their translator said they saw the star a few months ago. You know what? Gather all babies born in the last two years. Round them all up and kill them!

Yehudah: Kill them?!

Herod: Why are you so damn surprised?
Are you hiding them from me?

Yehudah: No, my lord!
It's just that, this could be God's chosen . . .

Herod: Enough! Guards! Arrest this man and kill him along with these kings! No King will come from Bethlehem under my watch! Now go and find out which virgins and priests knew this King.

Yehudah: Lord! Have mercy on me!

This murder in Bethlehem fulfilled the prophecy,

Jeremiah:

"A voice in Ramah was heard crying.
Tears flowed with much mourning.
Rachel cried and refused consolation,
for all her children are dead."

Time Stamp   :   25 February 4 BC
Location Stamp   :   Goshen, Egypt

50

The Holy Family arrived and looked for a place to settle.

Time Stamp   : 5 March 4 BC
Location Stamp   : Jerusalem, Palestinia

It has been months since Herod's symptoms started. Around this time, it turned for the worse.

Bnyakob: Did you hear about Herod?

Alex: Yeah, I heard from the son of Saripheus that his evil has gotten worse.

Bnyakob: You mean, you believe
            the rumours from Bethlehem?

Alex: What rumours? I'm referring to his illness.

Bnyakob: Of course, of course. I think he deserves it.

Alex: Right? That must be a punishment
            for that monstrous . . . animal!

Bnyakob: The temple! Of all places!

Alex: What did the priests say about it?

Bnyakob: They couldn't say no to Herod. If he can dispose
            of the high priest, he can dispose all of them.

Alex: Maybe we should be the one to take action.

Bnyakob: This is what you get for listening
            to the son of Saripheus.

Alex: Nope, Matthias agrees.
I think it's a worthy cause.

Bnyakob: Are you saying you are willing to die to *lowers voice* take down Herod's bird?

Alex: The eagle at the temple!
Don't say it like that! Hahaha!

Bnyakob: Hahaha. Of course, I'm referring to that abomination. But I don't know . . .

Alex: I think it would set a good example for any future leader who wish to desecrate God's temple.

Bnyakob: Maybe we should do it
to set the example for our people.

Alex: There you go!

Bnyakob: But die? I don't know . . .

Time Stamp   : 6 March 4 BC
Location Stamp : Jerusalem, Palestinia

Herod receives a letter from Caesar giving him a freehand to decide on his treacherous son's fate. Antipater was behind bars inside the same building that time.

Time Stamp   : 7 March 4 BC
Location Stamp : Jerusalem, Palestinia

Waves of pain assaulted Herod and this time, he could not take it anymore. He ordered everyone in his court to leave him alone. As soon as everyone was out, he took out a knife . . .

Achiabus: Herod! No!

Herod: Let me die!!

The cry was heard all over the palace down to the prison below.

Antipater: What was that? Is that my father?

Warden: You will know as soon as word reach here.

Antipater: Tell you what, let me out of here. I am the heir to
               the throne. I can reward your deed handsomely.

Warden: . . .

Antipater: Generously! How much do you want? Just get me
               out of this prison now!

Back in Herod's court . . .

Priest: He seems fine now.

Achiabus: Thank you. Please excuse us.

Herod: Why don't you just let me die?
               sobs
               This pain is unbearable.

Achiabus: You know, there is news of a certain oasis in
               Callirrhoe that reputedly cures even those that
               were deemed impossible to treat.

Herod: You know what, take me there.

Birth and Childhood

Time Stamp   :   9 March 4 BC
Location Stamp   :   Callirrhoe, in modern-day Jordan

Achiabus: This is a hot spring, okay?
                        This could possibly hurt.

Herod: I don't care. If it heals me, it heals me. If it kills
                        me . . . die, die lor.

Outside of the oasis . . .

Nabbatean #1: Why is there a queue today?

Nabbatean #2: It seems that the king is here.

Nabbatean #1: Herod? I thought he's dead.

Nabbatean #2: By the look of those guards,
                        it seems he is here and is alive.

A cry was heard all over the oasis
followed by howls that tapered off.

Nabbatean #1: What was that?

Nabbatean #2: If Herod was alive, he is dead by now.

Time Stamp   :   11 March 4 BC
Location Stamp   :   Herod's Palace, Jericho

Priest: He's asleep now.

Achiabus: Does it look like he will recover?

Priest: *shakes head*

Life & Works of Jesus

:   Somewhere in Jerusalem

Matthias: Now is the time, my brothers. That tyrant is in the mercy of God. Now is the time to take down this abomination!

Alex: Down with the tyrant! Down with the eagle!

Bnyakob: But what if he's still alive? What if he sends his heirs to arrest and possibly kill us?

Judas: We will all eventually die. But if we can, shouldn't we choose a good reason to die? Should we live a rich long life and die of old age, or live a short life full of virtue?

Matthias: If we will die taking down this abomination, we will die trying to preserve the law of our ancestors! This deed assures us of immortality, not only in this generation but also forever! Remember the 12 martyrs in the book of Maccabeus? Remember the deeds of that great family that freed us from those Greeks pigs?

Judas: It is a fitting conclusion for us who love virtue to meet death with praise and honour. This kind of death is so, so, so worth it. We do not die out of old age as cowards to God's standards. We die by acts of braveness! Like soldiers.

Alex: Yeah!

Judas: Like the legendary soldiers of David!

<u>O</u>thers:	Yeah!
<u>B</u>nyakob:	Alex, this is dangerous.
<u>A</u>lex:	Why are you so afraid? Think of the reputation we'll leave behind for our children and relatives. Think of the conviction we will inspire and leave behind!
<u>B</u>nyakob:	When are we doing this?
<u>A</u>lex:	Tomorrow at the Fast of Esther.

Time Stamp   : 12 March 4 BC, Fast of Esther
Location Stamp : Temple of Jerusalem

Herod's guards arrested a group of over 40 young men who attacked the temple and chopped down his golden bird.

Time Stamp   : 13 March 4 BC, Purim
Location Stamp : Herod's Palace, Jericho

<u>H</u>erod:	Will the eclipse be visible here?
<u>H</u>ead Minister:	Our astrologers said so.
<u>H</u>erod:	That's something to look forward to.
<u>H</u>ead Minister:	Your majesty, may I call your attention to another matter.
<u>H</u>erod:	You sure have plenty of news today. Go on.
<u>H</u>ead Minister:	A group of young men were arrested for vandalising your tribute to the Temple.

Herod: Vandalise? How?

Head Minister: By chopping it down.

Herod: Chop it down?!

Head Minister: With axes.

Herod: I don't think you can chop it down upright. That huge thing will kill them when it falls on their head.

Head Minister: Actually . . . they pulled it down first.

Herod: I don't think a dozen men can pull down such a huge statue.

Head Minister: *nervous laughter* Your majesty, I think I forgot to mention that there was actually a mob.

Herod: Mob?

Head Minister: The mob pulled it down and started chopping it, but when your soldiers came, only 40 people were arrested.

Herod: Were you able to arrest their leaders?

Head Minister: It seems we got all of them.
                   Two, matter of fact.

Herod: Who were they?

Head Minister: Matthias and Judas

Herod: Matthias the high priest?

Head Minister: No, your majesty.
Some guy who seems to be popular in Jerusalem.

Herod: Don't they know that eagle was dedicated to the temple? Did they not realise that they have committed a crime against God?

Head Minister: . . .

Herod: And what did the high priest do?

Head Minister: It seems he was ill when it happened.

Herod: Give me a list of candidates for the high priesthood . . . No, give me the name of one of his relatives. I want him to burn with regret!

Head Minister: *bows*

Herod: Tie the rebels at the plaza. You know how. I will address them as you prepare the decorations.

Later that day, a group of young men were burned alive. Herod stripped Matthias of his office and gave it to Josephus, his relative.

Head Minister: Your majesty, there is one other matter that you need to know of.

Herod: If this is not important, I do not want to hear about it.

Head Minister: It concerns your son, Antipater.

Herod: Why? Did he escape?

Head Minister: I have the jailer here to report what transpired.

Herod: . . . Well? Speak!

Warden: Your majesty, about a week ago when we heard a
                  cry in your palace in Jerusalem, rumour got out
                  that you died, and Antipater got wind of it.

Herod: Go on.

Warden: He bribed me to set him free . . .

Herod: And you dared to release him?

Warden: No, your majesty. I denied him such. He is still
                  imprisoned. I came here because I think you
                  should know.

Herod: Give this man . . . something for his trouble.

Head Minister: *bows*

Herod: And kill Antipater. Pronto! *falls down*

Head Minister: Your majesty! You, go get help. Quick!!

Time Stamp   : 15 March 4 BC
Location Stamp   : Herod's Palace, Jericho

Planning to make the world feel the pain of his death, Herod gave
orders to summon the nobility.

Salome: You heard the king. Send out the invitations.

Head Minister: *bows*

The Branch went to Branch Town   **19**
(Mt 2:15, 19–23; Lk 2:39b, 2:1b)

Time Stamp   : 17 March 4 BC
Location Stamp : Goshen, Egypt

An angel of God appeared to Joseph in a dream.

Revi'imalak: Those who were trying to kill the Child are dead.
                Go and take them back now.

That morning . . .

Joseph: Dear, I had a dream last night.

Mary: Please share.

Joseph: It seems Herod is dead.

Mary: Seems?

Joseph: An angel of the Lord appeared in my dream and
                said those who were trying to kill the Child are
                dead.

Mary: Hosannah!

Joseph: Indeed! We can head back now.

Khufuiah: Stay for a few more days. That should allow us to prepare you for your journey.

Time Stamp   : 18 March 4 BC
Location Stamp : Herod's Palace, Jericho

Archelaus: I will head out to Jerusalem after we lay my father's remains in Herodium.

Antipas: What made you think you are the next king?

Archelaus: Abba said so in his will.
Were you not paying attention?

Antipas: Oh no, you don't. I will have the throne when Caesar ratifies my position.

Archelaus: You wouldn't dare.

Antipas: You'll see.

Time Stamp   : 26 March 4 BC
Location Stamp : Herod's Palace, Jericho

Antipas is celebrating his new position as king
after a period of mourning.

Salome: What are you going to do about your brother? He is the name written in the will.

Antipas: I know what you did to the nobles, Salome. How would I know you were not sent here to keep me in check? It is wise if you choose to support me instead.

Birth and Childhood

Salome: . . .

Philip: You know what our father wanted, right?

Antipas: For you to disobey him, makes me wonder how
                  much of his last will was changed. Brother, how
                  would I know if you're not with her in this? You
                  weren't exactly in good terms with father before
                  he died.

Salome: Look, your brother is in Jerusalem right now,
                  winning the people.

Antipas: It will mean nothing
                  if Caesar gives me his blessing.

Salome: How do you plan to do that?

Antipas: One way or another.

Philip: If you plan to go to Rome,
                  I will come with you.

Antipas: Bro, I got this. But tonight, tomorrow, and for as
                  long as we like, we'll keep celebrating. For this is
                  a great day for us and Israel!

Philip/Salome: Cheers!

Time Stamp   : 27 March 4 BC
Location Stamp   : Goshen, Egypt

Joseph: Mary! The news confirms it!

Mary:	What news?
Joseph:	Herod is dead!
Mary:	We can go back to Bethlehem now. Praise God!
Joseph:	Exile is not the life fit for the King.
Khufuiah:	I heard the news from merchants who came from the north. I guess the time is ripe.
Joseph:	If we prepare now, we can make it to Passover.
Mary:	Yes please.
Khufuiah:	I'll have the servants tie up the provisions to your mule.

Joseph obeyed and went back to Israel and so fulfilled what God said through His prophet.

Hosea:

"I CALLED MY SON OUT OF EGYPT."

~ Living God

Time Stamp   : 10 April 4 BC
Location Stamp : Herod's Palace, Jerusalem

The Jews were resisting the claim of Archelaus to the throne and were divided on the reforms he has proposed. A group of soldiers were sent to the temple earlier where people are in the middle of their cleansing ritual.

Head Minister: Master, the mob killed the soldiers
you sent to the temple.

Archelaus: They really are pushing it. If they would not respect the reforms I offer and the tolerance I have been showing them, then I have no choice.

Head Minister: . . .

Archelaus: They will now see the fury of Herod!

Head Minister: But, master, what if Caesar finds your actions presumptive of the position he hasn't confirmed.

Archelaus: I am the rightful heir to the throne, do you doubt me? Or are you here to spy for my brother?

Head Minister: Goodness! Lord, God forbid. *kneels*

Archelaus: Send a full fist into that mob.
They will accept my leadership even if it means flooding the streets with their blood!

Head Minister: As you wish, my Lord.

Location Stamp   : On the road to Bethlehem, Palestinia

Joseph: Mary, I got a dream again last night.

Mary: You look troubled. Was it bad?

Joseph:	More like a warning.
Mary:	Any details?
Joseph:	We'll act when we find out more.

They went back to the inn where they stayed before.

Bet:	Praise God you are all safe!
Mary:	Look! He has the sweetest smile.
Bet:	The Lord's smile brings me peace.
Joseph:	I am sorry. I heard about what happened.
Bet:	Do not worry about us. We . . .
Jonathan:	It is terrible!
Bet:	Calm down! We have guests. Have a seat. Do you remember them?
Jonathan:	Pardon me but this is urgent. Archelaus just killed 3,000 pilgrims at the temple. Earlier, the people killed his first squad of soldiers, but a bigger detachment came and killed everyone in the temple. *breaks down*
Bet:	Lord, have mercy!
Joseph:	We cannot endanger the life of the Lord. We must travel north.

	We'll take the route to Caesarea to avoid Jerusalem.
<u>Bet</u>:	Hold on, Joseph. Jonathan, come! We need to help them get out of here fast.
Mary:	Where shall we go?
Joseph:	We'll be safe in Galilee. Our people will be happy to hide us.
Mary:	What about Jesus?
Joseph:	We can't let others know that the Heir to the Throne is alive. Our Sovereign God will hide Him the way He hid Jehoash from Athaliah.
Mary:	My King, why do you need to hide like David?

They headed back to Galilee and settled in Nazareth where Mary first received the news from the angel. This fulfilled what the prophets hinted,

"A shoot will come from Jesse
and a Branch (ve•Netzer) will shoot from his roots"

~ Isaiah (11:1)

Also,

"...the Boy will be a nazirite (ne•Zir)..."

~ Judges (13:7)

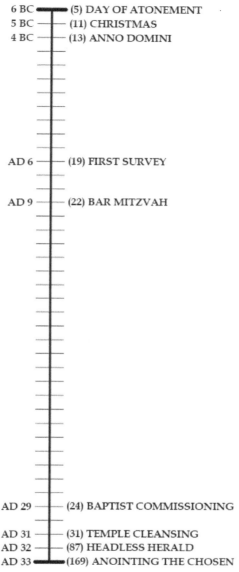

6 BC — (5) DAY OF ATONEMENT

5 BC — (11) CHRISTMAS

4 BC — (13) ANNO DOMINI

AD 6 — (19) FIRST SURVEY

AD 9 — (22) BAR MITZVAH

AD 29 — (24) BAPTIST COMMISSIONING

AD 31 — (31) TEMPLE CLEANSING

AD 32 — (87) HEADLESS HERALD

AD 33 — (169) ANOINTING THE CHOSEN

Timeline showing the Life of Christ from the events starting from His conception all the way to His death The relevant event numbers are indicated with a short-form of the title (19 – SURVEY is event 19 when Quirinius conducted his survey).

Time Stamp   : AD 6
Location Stamp   : Judea, Palestinia

Archelaus was deposed by Rome. Quirinius, the new governor of Syria, announced to everyone who used to fall under the jurisdiction of Archelaus that Augustus Caesar ordered everyone to register. Everyone went to register. Joseph, Mary, and Jesus can now visit Jerusalem safely.

Herald in the Wilderness   20
(Lk 1:80)

Johannes grew up strong in spirit. Later in life, he lived in a desert near Judea referred to as, "the wilderness", and stayed there before he appeared to Israel.

Holy Boy   21
(Lk 2:40)

In Nazareth, Jesus grew strong and wise with God's grace.

teachers meet & greet The Teacher   22
(Lk 2:41–51)

Time Stamp   : 17 April AD 9
Location Stamp   : Nazareth, Galilee

The parents of Jesus believed in God and obeyed Him. As such, the whole family heads to Jerusalem every year to celebrate Passover.

Time Stamp   : 19 April to 4 May AD 9,
                          Passover until the end
                          of the Feast of Unleavened Bread
Location Stamp   : Jerusalem, Judea

Joseph and Mary travelled with the whole family to Jerusalem since the law required every Jew to attend. Jesus is now twelve and as accustomed, they stayed in Jerusalem until the celebration was over.

Time Stamp   : 5 May AD 9
Location Stamp : Jerusalem, Judea

On the way back to Nazareth, Mary and Joseph did not realise Jesus stayed behind. It's completely normal to entrust your child to the care of your relatives' when travelling because kids often played together.

Time Stamp   : 7 May AD 9
Location Stamp : Nazareth, Galilee

As soon as they reached Nazareth, they realised Jesus didn't stay with any of their relatives. After checking the neighbours and relatives, they decided to head back to Jerusalem.

Time Stamp   : 10 May AD 9
Location Stamp : Jerusalem, Judea

Three days later, which was about six days from the time they left Jerusalem, they found Jesus in the temple, sitting among religious teachers and actively interacting with them. As they excused Him from the gathering, the teachers and spectators told them how amazing the answers of Jesus were.

Mary: My Child, we were distressed
            to find you missing.
            We looked for you everywhere!
            Why have You done this to us?

Jesus: *Search for Me? Why did you search? Didn't you know that I must be in My Father's house?*

This was Jesus' first recorded statement. He then went to Nazareth with His parents. Mary treasured all these things in her heart.

Santo Niño obeys   23
(Lk 2:52)

Jesus grew up obedient to His parents, wise, and favoured by God and people.

MARK

1	2	3	4
5	6	7	8
9	10	11	12
13	14	15	16

JOHN

1	2	3	4	5	6	7
8	9	10	11	12	13	14
15	16	17	18	19	20	21

MATTHEW

1	2	3	4	5	6	7
8	9	10	11	12	13	14
15	16	17	18	19	20	21
22	23	24	25	26	27	28

LUKE

1	2	3	4	5	6
7	8	9	10	11	12
13	14	15	16	17	18
19	20	21	22	23	24

A chart showing all chapters of each Gospel. The shading indicates the progress of the narrative with respect to each chapter and book. A shading of Matthew 1 & 2 means it has been completed at the end of this book's chapter.

Chapter 3

Baptism and Pre-ministry

Johannes was simply a witness to Jesus.
Jesus is the True Light that gives light to everyone.
Jesus is coming!

~ John

Your Mission: Identify the Baptiser   24
(Jn 1:33b; Lk 3:1–2; Mt 3:1, 4–5; Mk 1:5a)

Time Stamp   : AD 29 (sometime before 19 January AD 31)
Location Stamp   : Wilderness, Judea

These were the rulers of the region
around the ancient land of Israel:
Tiberius Caesar is on the 15th year of his reign
as emperor of Rome.
Pontius Pilate was governor of Judea.
Herod Antipas was ruler of Galilee.
Philip, Herod's brother, was ruler of Iturea and Traconitis.
Lysanias was ruler of Abilene.
Annas and Caiaphas were the high priests.

God sent Johannes the Baptist
to tell everyone who Jesus is
so everyone can believe.

~ John

Location Stamp   : Wilderness, Judea

It was around this time when our man Johannes bar (son of) Zechariah received a message from God. He was living in the wilderness at that time. He wore a garment made of camel hair tied with a leather belt. He ate a diet of locusts and wild honey.

God:

FIND OUT WHO WILL BAPTISE WITH THE HOLY SPIRIT BY WASHING WITH WATER. YOU WILL KNOW THE ONE WHEN YOU SEE THE SPIRIT DESCEND AND REST ON THAT PERSON.

Johannes: Will it be David's Son?

. . .

Johannes: Is that Person the Messiah, the King?

. . .

Johannes: Will He be the prophet like Moses?

. . .

Johannes: How about the Lamb You promised to provide?

. . .

Johannes: I don't remember anything in the Scripture that talked about the Spirit...

Oh, Joel. Right.
Wait, did You not say You will do that?

. . .

Location Stamp : Jordan River, Palestinia

Johannes obeyed, went out, and preached on both sides of the Jordan River. People of Judea, Jerusalem, and the Jordan Valley came to see and hear him.

"Unless I wash you . . ." ~ Jesus

Herald Goes to Work   25
(Mt 3:2–3, 6–12; Mk 1:2–8; Lk 3:3–18; Jn 1:19–28, 33b)

Malachi:

"LOOK, I SENT MY MESSENGER AHEAD TO PREPARE MY WAY."

~ God Almighty

Isaiah:

"Prepare the Way of the Lord! Straighten His path!
All valleys will be filled and all highlands levelled.
Bends will be straightened and rough roads smoothed.
Then, all people will see God's salvation."'

- voice shouting from the wilderness

Location Stamp : Jordan River, Palestinia

Johannes: Change! For the Kingdom of Heaven is near.

Come and I will wash you with water.
This is a life-changing baptism
for the forgiveness of your sins.

76

And so he did. Those who confess their sins were washed in the Jordan River.

Location Stamp   : Al-Maghtas / Bethabara - beyond the Jordan River

Jewish leaders sent priests, Pharisees, Sadducees, and Temple assistants from Jerusalem to watch him baptise.

Shaal: Who are you?

Johannes: If you are wondering if I am the Messiah,
                no, I am not.

Bea: Are you the Prophet we are expecting,
                the one like Moses?

Johannes: No

Shaal: Then who are you?
                We need something to report
                to those who sent us.
                Who do you think you are?

Johannes: I am that voice in the wilderness
                that Isaiah wrote about

Naftali: You mean, God is coming?
                So, you are Elijah!

Johannes: No, I'm not Elijah.

Bea: If you aren't the Messiah, the Prophet, or Elijah,
                what right do you have to wash people?

Johannes: God sent me to baptise with water. He said,

> **"FIND OUT WHO WILL BAPTISE**
> **WITH THE HOLY SPIRIT**
> **BY BAPTISING WITH WATER.**
> **YOU WILL KNOW THE ONE**
> **WHEN YOU SEE THE SPIRIT DESCEND**
> **AND REST ON THAT PERSON."**

Silencing them, he then denounced them and the crowds.

Johannes: You snake eggs!
              Who warned you to escape God's wrath?

Bnabraam: We're not the Serpent's children!
              Our father is Abraham, we'll be fine.

Johannes: Just because you are Abraham's children
              does not guarantee a safe pass! I tell you,
              God can make children for Abraham
              out of these stones.

              Even now, the axe sits next to the tree.
              All trees that do not produce good fruit
              will be chopped down and burned.
              Prove your repentance with results!

Strephos: What should people like us do?

Johannes: Give all your excess to the poor.
              Food or clothing, give them to the poor.

Gabbaim: Teacher, what should tax collectors like us do?

Johannes:	Collect the exact amount of tax required. No more, no less.
Chayal:	What should soldiers like us do?
Johannes:	Do not extort. Do not accuse falsely. Be content with your salary.

Everyone was expecting the Messiah's imminent arrival, and they were wondering if Johannes is the Messiah.

Andrew:	He must be the new Moses because he baptised us.
Simon:	How is washing related to the new Moses?
John:	Well, the new Moses should do a little of what he did, like when he commanded the people to wash themselves to prepare to meet God.
Johannes:	Those who repent of their sins and turn to God I will wash with water, but soon, Someone greater is coming. So great that I'm not even worthy to remove nor carry that Person's shoes.
John:	One greater than a king? So that would be the Messiah, the Son of David!

79

But how can He be greater than you
when you came first?

Johannes: No, that Person existed before I did.
That Person could be in this crowd,
seemingly ordinary like everyone else,
unrecognisable.

John: Existed before you? What does that mean?

Simon: Is there a way to recognise Him?

Johannes: I immerse you with water, but That Person
will submerge you in the Holy Spirit!

Yes, baptise you
with the Holy Spirit
and with fire!

That Person is bent on separating
what's useful from what is useless.

After cleaning up, what's useful will be kept
while the ones discarded will be razed
on flames that never die.

Johannes warned everyone whenever he announces the Gospel.

Johannes:

Prepare the Way of the Lord! Straighten His path!
All valleys will be filled and all highlands levelled.
Bends will be straightened and rough roads smoothed.
Then, all people will see God's salvation.

ANNO DOMINI 31

(26) TRINITY REVEALED	TEMPTATION	(30) CANA	(31) TEMPLE CLEANSING
19 JANUARY 7 SHEBET	FEBRUARY ADAR I	13 MARCH 30 ADAR I	18 APRIL 7 NISAN
(35) BAPTIST ARRESTED	(48) FISHERS OF MEN	(52) WHY FAST?	(57) SERMON
3 MAY 22 NISAN	3 JUNE 23 IYAR	26 JULY 17 TAMMUZ	12 AUGUST 5 AV
(67) KINGDOM OF GOD	FEAST OF TABERNACLES	TOUR	(84) WANTED: WORKERS
16 SEPTEMBER 10 ELUL	OCTOBER TISHRI	NOVEMBER HESHVAN	19 DECEMBER 15 KISLEV

Calendar of the year AD 31. The relevant event numbers are indicated with a short-form of the title (26 – TRINITY REVEALED is event 26 when the first record of the Trinity was witnessed). Equivalent Jewish month is likewise indicated.

Trinity Spotted! 26
(Mt 3:13–17; Mk 1:9–11; Lk 3:21–22; Jn 1:32)

The world did not recognise Him.

~ John

Who will Baptise?

Time Stamp   : Friday, 19 January AD 31 (Shebat 7)
Location Stamp : Jordan River, Judea

One day, Jesus came from Nazareth, Galilee, to the Jordan River.

Mary:	John! What are you doing here?
John:	Hi Auntie! I am here to help the Baptist out. Hey Jesus! How you doin?
Jesus:	*smiles*
Mary:	Oh! So, you are a disciple of Johannes. Did you know the Baptist is your cousin?
John:	Yes, Mom told me.
Mary:	Of course, of course. Are your parents here?
John:	No, after their baptism, they went back to Galilee with James.
Mary:	I see. Could you take us to your cousin?
John:	I'd be honoured!

Johannes was baptising the crowd when he saw his cousin approaching. Remembering his mother's stories, he welcomed Him.

Mary:	Greetings, Johannes!
Johannes:	Auntie! I didn't expect you. What brings you here?
Mary:	We came to be baptised. Isn't that your message?
Johannes:	Why come to me? Jesus should be the One washing me!
Everyone:	*laughs*
Jesus:	*For now, we follow the right way -* that is, you must obey God and wash Me.
Johannes:	Right, of course I should! Come!

How is the Anointed anointed?

As soon as Jesus got up and broke the water, Johannes saw heaven open and the Spirit of God descend in a physical body that looked like a dove and perched on Him. While Jesus was praying, Johannes heard a Voice from heaven address Jesus.

God:

"YOU BRING ME GREAT JOY, MY DEAR SON."

Johannes: !!

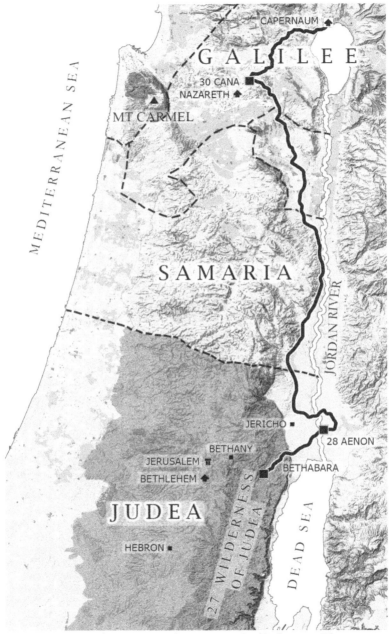

From Fasting to Feasting. From Suffering to Glory.

Did God really say. . .?

- the serpent

Temptation Proof 27
(Mt 4:1–11; Mk 1:12–13; Lk 4:1–13)

The Holy Spirit Moves

Time Stamp	:	20 January AD 31 (day 1)
Location Stamp	:	Wilderness, Judea

Jesus came out of the Jordan River full of the Holy Spirit. The Spirit led Jesus to the wilderness of Judea where He was out among wild animals for forty days and forty nights. In those days, He did not eat anything.

Temptation #1: Need

Hungry after His fast, the devil came and tempted Him.

> Devil: If You are the Son of God,
> speak so that these stones can turn to bread.

> Jesus: *It has been said and written that,*
>
> *"Humans do not live by bread alone,*
> *but by every word*
> *that comes from the mouth of God."*

Temptation #2: Testing versus Trusting God

Then the tempter took Him to the holy city, Jerusalem, to the top of the temple.

85

Devil: If You are the Son of God,
leap down! For it is inscribed,

"for You, He will order His angels.
With their hands they will hold You
so, You won't get hurt."

Jesus: *It is also inscribed,*

"Do not test YHWH your God."

Temptation #3: Source of Power

Again, the devil then took Him to a tall tall mountain and showed Him all the world's kingdoms and their glory in one go.

Devil: All these were given to me and anyone I pass it to. I'll give You all these kingdoms, their glory, and the authority to rule them if You will drop down and worship me.

Jesus: *Leave, Satan! It is inscribed,*

"Worship YHWH your God and serve no one else."

Jesus 1 – Devil 0

Time Stamp : 7 March AD 31 (day 40 ends at 6:00 p.m.)
Location Stamp : Wilderness, Judea

After tempting Jesus, Satan went away to wait for his next chance. Angels arrived and took care of Him.

"Lamb of God is . . ." ~ Herald

28

(Jn 1:29–31, 34)

> *God sent Johannes the Baptist*
> *to tell everyone who Jesus is*
> *so everyone can believe.*

~ John

Time Stamp   : 8 March AD 31 (day 41)
Location Stamp   : Jordan River, Judea

The Baptist saw Jesus coming towards him, possibly gaunt.

Johannes: Look! The Lamb of God
who takes away the sin of the world!

Philip: What did you just say?
How did you describe Him?

Johannes: When I said,

"Someone greater is coming,
because He existed before I did."
I was referring to Him.

I didn't know He was the Christ,
but He is the very reason
I baptised with water
so Israel will know.

Shikor: How did you know it was Him?

Johannes: After I dipped Him in the water,
He came up,

and I saw the Holy Spirit
perch on Him from heaven
in a body that looked like a dove.

I didn't know
He's the Baptiser of the Holy Spirit
but when God commissioned me
to baptise with water,

He said,

"YOU WILL KNOW WHO WILL BAPTISE
WITH THE HOLY SPIRIT
WHEN YOU SEE THE SPIRIT DESCEND
AND REST ON THAT PERSON."

Nathanael: The Spirit of God!?
The One that empowered Samson
and gave wisdom to Solomon?

Johannes: Yes, THE Holy Spirit!
Not only that, but while He was praying,
I also heard a Voice from heaven say,

"YOU BRING ME GREAT JOY, MY DEAR SON."

~ Almighty God

Philip: You saw all this?

Johannes: I did, so I confirm
that He is the Son of God.

Nathanael: The Son . . .

Part 1: The First Disciples?

29

(Jn 1:35–51)

The Two Disciples of Johannes

Time Stamp   : 9 March AD 31 (day 42)
Location Stamp : Jordan River, Judea

Johannes stood next to his two disciples, Andrew and John, when he saw Jesus walked by.

Johannes:	Look! The Lamb of God!
John:	The same Lamb you saw in your vision?
Johannes:	The same One I baptised sometime last month.
John:	Wait!! Isn't that Jesus?
Johannes:	Yes! Our cousin is the Chosen One.
John:	What?!
Andrew:	You know Him?
John:	Yes, but I . . .
Andrew:	And how is He your cousin?
John:	Well, my mom is His mother's sister.
Andrew:	Won't you introduce me?
John:	I don't know what to say!

Andrew: You must introduce me! Come, I'll make something up.

John: But...

Andrew: Just come!

When Jesus turned and saw them following, He asked,

Jesus: *What do you want?*

Andrew: Rabbi, we wondered where You are staying?

Jesus: *Come and see.*

They reached the place where He stayed around 4:00 p.m. and they hanged out with Him for the rest of the day.

Cornerstone meets the Rock

Time Stamp   : Evening of 9 March AD 31. A little past 6:00 p.m.

Andrew later went out to look for his brother, Simon.

Simon: Calm down! 'Sup?

Andrew: We've found the Messiah! Come! Come!

Simon: John, are you two pranking me?

John: I don't even know if I'm the one being pranked Haha!

Heading back to Jesus . . .

Andrew: Good evening, Rabbi! I came back to introduce
               you to my brother, Simon.

Jesus looked at Simon.

Jesus: *Simon son of Iōannou,*
               you will be called Cephas.

First Disciples!!

Time Stamp   : Saturday, 10 March AD 31 (day 43)
Location Stamp : Jordan River, Judea

Mary: Jesus, remember the wedding? John told me Your
               Aunt Salome will be coming from Bethsaida too.
               We need to be in Galilee before it starts. We'll
               leave after Sabbath.

Jesus went out.

Andrew: His mom told us how He was born! I was blown
               away!

Philip: So, He is the son of Joseph, a descendant of
               David. So that makes Him the heir to the throne!

Andrew: Yes!

Philip: And all this time, He was in Nazareth?

Andrew: Yes!

Simon (Peter): Guys! Guys! He's approaching!

Philip: You! I remember You! You're the Lamb whom the Baptist identified.

Andrew: Greetings, Rabbi! Please meet our friend, Philip. He's also from Bethsaida.

Jesus: *Follow Me.*

Simon (Peter):   Whoah!

Andrew: He's calling you to be His disciple!

Philip: Yes, Rabbi! My answer is yes!

Jesus: Call your friend. We're heading out.

Philip: You mean, these two?

Jesus: They are my cousin's disciples. I'm referring to the one under a fig tree at the outskirts of Bethany on a hill facing Jerusalem.

Philip went out and got surprised to find Nathanael.

Philip: This is way too far from the river. This is borderline close to a Sabbath day's walk! Which weirdo would hide in this . . . Nathanael?

Nathanael: Philip! How did you find me?

Philip: Uhm, do you remember the guy the Baptist called the Lamb of God?

Nathanael: The Son of God?

Philip: It's Jesus, son of Joseph. We found Him! Apparently, He's from Nazareth.

Nathanael: Nazareth?! Can anything good come out of Nazareth?

Philip: See for yourself.

While approaching Jesus, Philip was sharing Andrew's stories to Nathanael.

Simon (Peter): So when Johannes saw You at the river, You just came from fasting?

Andrew: For forty days? Is that right?

Jesus: *Look! Here is a true Israelite.*
No nonsense through and through.

Nathanael: How did You know me?

Jesus: *I saw you under your secret fig tree, and yes,*
I saw you before Philip found you.

Nathanael:

Rabbi!
You
are
the Son
of
God!

The
King
of
Israel!

Jesus: *If this is enough to make you believe,*
               you've seen nothing yet.

               I assure you,
               you will all see heaven open
               and watch angels of God
               serve the Son of Man.

The Week in Cana   30
(Jn 2:1–12)

Time Stamp   : 13 March AD 31 (day 46)
Location Stamp : Cana, Galilee

James: Philip, is that you?

Philip: James! John!
                You remember Nathanael my friend?

James: Yes. Good to see you again, Nathanael.

Philip: What brings you here?

James: We're invited to the wedding, duh?

Philip: Haha! Of course, of course. Did you two come
                here by yourselves?

James: Our parents were the ones invited.

Nathanael: Must be the wedding of the century. Look, everyone is here, from the high priest and their relatives to prominent rabbis, textile and incense traders, even tax collectors! Look, John, it's Nicodemus!

John: Oh yeah, it is! By the way, how did you get invited? I mean, which of the couple did you know?

Nathanael: None. The "*Rabbi*" invited us.

John: Rabbi? Which one?

Philip: The One that Johannes called
the Lamb of God.

John: Jesus? Jesus, son of Joseph?

Philip: Yes. Why? Don't you know your cousin?

John: I do, but why did He invite you?

Philip: We're His disciples now.

John: What?!? How?

Elsewhere in the celebration . . .

Salome: John told me!

Mary: Greetings, sister and Zebedee!

Salome: You never told me!

Mary: I don't want to endanger you! You know how we had to beg off our visits to Jerusalem when Archelaus was still in power.

Salome: How come Elizabeth knew?

Mary: Come, I'll tell you all about it.

Time Stamp   : Sometime in the middle of the banquet, 16-20 March AD 31. Possibly Sunday, 18 March.

A sound of breaking jars was heard near Mary and Salome.

Zebedee: Oh no! That sounded like a lot of jars.

Mary: Let's go and check.

The three looked at the sight of broken jars in horror.

Naaman: My lady, all the wine jars broke! We're gonna die!

Zebedee: Tsk! Tsk! Tsk! This wedding is doomed!

Salome: I'm not sure the village has enough wine to cover the remaining days. With this much important guests, the couple will end up…

Naaman: We're all gonna die!

Mary: Don't say that. Don't tell the groom yet and order your people to clean this up. You, come with me.

Mary went out and looked for Jesus.

Mary: They ran out of wine.

Jesus: *What does that mean to you and Me?*

Mary: These people need help.

Jesus: *Woman, My time hasn't come.*

Mary thought for a moment what Jesus meant,
then glanced at Naaman.

Mary: Do whatever He tells you.

Jesus: Show Me where your earthen jars are.

Naaman took Jesus where the only jars in the celebration are.

Salome: Does Jesus know where to get wine out here?

Mary: Remember one of our favourite stories?

Salome: The one about Rahab? Rachel? Ruth?
Which one?

Mary: No, I was referring to the one with Elijah.

Salome: Are you bringing this up
because his name is Naaman?

Mary: No, I was referring to the one
where the widow . . .

Near the entrance where people wash,

Naaman:	These are the only jars we have. All our wine jars are broken.
Abdias:	Naaman, we can't carry these jars! They're made of stone. They're huge, and I don't think we can haul them fast enough when they're full!
Naaman:	I know, but we need to hurry.
Abdias:	Master, are Your wine merchants nearby?
Jesus:	*Fill the jars with water.*
Abdias:	These jars have about 80-120 litres each. It usually takes us all day to fill up all six!
Naaman:	Get everyone free to help. Double time!

As soon as one of the jars were filled to the brim . . .

Jesus:	*Serve it and give one to the emcee.*
Naaman:	Alma, you don't look sweaty. Here, fill one pitcher and pour some to the emcee. Naarah, get another pitcher and start serving the tables. Where's Qatan?
Jesus:	You can stop as soon as all six jars are filled.

The master of ceremonies sipped the cup and tasted wine. Naaman saw the emcee's eyes open wide from afar.

Emcee:	Wow! This is superb! Where's that groom? Tell him to come over.

Alma: Right away, sir.

Everyone saw the groom walk up to the emcee and looked at what the two guys were doing.

Emcee: Hosts always, always serve the best wine first because guests won't complain if they get cheap wine when they're drunk. You weirdo! Haha! Why did you save the best for last?

The confused groom laughed and smiled.

Groom: Alma, pour me one and call Naaman over.

Naaman ran up as soon as he saw his master look his way.

Groom: What's going on?
                This isn't the wine we got from Oxus!

Naaman: Master, you must know . . .

While Naaman explained what happened, everyone at the banquet were all smiles, enjoying the new batch of wine.

Groom: Water?!

Emcee: What water? What's up?

Everyone was looking at the animate conversation of the two fellows as the people near them picked up the story and started passing around how Jesus turned water into wine.

Shikor: This came from the washing jar?

Alma:	Yes, lord, but . . .
Shikor:	No, no, no! This is the best wine I've ever had! Tell me where your master bought it.
Alma:	That Man told us to fetch water, and after the jars were filled, we were asked to serve it.
Shikor:	I know that Man!

Everyone went home from Cana mind blown at the miracle of Jesus. They wondered about the man who Johannes called Lamb of God, Taker of the world's sins, Baptiser of the Holy Spirit. These stories spread to all corners of Judea, Galilee, and other corners of the world, where guests came from and travelled about.

This is how Jesus first showed proof of His glory.

Salome:	Come with us to Bethsaida, you must tell me everything everything!
Mary:	We can't burden you too much. I know how busy you are.
Zebedee:	You can stay at Capernaum. There are nice inns there. Salome can visit you every day.

Time Stamp : 20 March AD 31
Location Stamp : Cana, Galilee

Jesus, His mother, some relatives, and two of His current disciples, Philip and Nathanael, went to Capernaum and stayed there for a few days.

MARK

1	2	3	4
5	6	7	8
9	10	11	12
13	14	15	16

JOHN

1	2	3	4	5	6	7
8	9	10	11	12	13	14
15	16	17	18	19	20	21

MATTHEW

1	2	3	4	5	6	7
8	9	10	11	12	13	14
15	16	17	18	19	20	21
22	23	24	25	26	27	28

LUKE

1	2	3	4	5	6
7	8	9	10	11	12
13	14	15	16	17	18
19	20	21	22	23	24

A chart showing all chapters of each Gospel. The shading indicates the progress of the narrative with respect to each chapter and book. A shading of Matthew 1, 2, and 3 means it has been completed at the end of this book's chapter.

Chapter 4

Passover #1

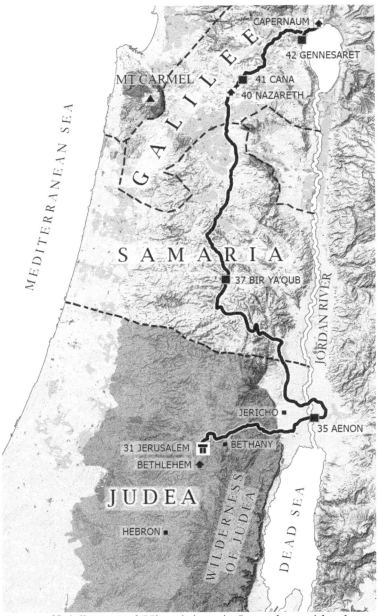

Jesus officially started His ministry in Jerusalem with a bang then headed to the dark where light is needed the most.

He came to His people but even they rejected Him.
To everyone else who receive Him
and believe in His Name,
He gave the right to become children of God.

~ John

Official Launch: Ministry of Jesus

Jesus was around 30 years old when His public ministry started.

Allegation #1: Destroy this Temple?? 31
(Jn 2:13–22)

Time Stamp   : 18 April AD 31
Location Stamp : Temple, Jerusalem

Jesus arrived in Jerusalem with enough time for everyone to go through the purification rituals before Passover.

Mary: Philip, can you help us pick some sacrificial animals for the purification ritual?

Philip: Yes, ma'am.
                Nathanael, do you mind coming with me?

Nathanael: Sure, let's go!

At the temple area, Jesus went with His disciples and stood outside watching while His disciples ran their errands.

Philip: Rabbi, the price of oxen and sheep are up. Even the rates of doves aren't cheap.

Nathanael: They wouldn't accept drachma either. We need to change our coins to the temple's coins, but the exchange rates are outrageous.

Philip: I feel sorry for the poor folk begging for cheaper rates. One old lady got back-slapped!

In His indignance, He made a whip out of ropes and chased everyone who sold sacrificial animals out of the temple. He drove them out including the animals.

Philip: Yikes! Look at all those animals go!

Nathanael: That sheep can't be sold anymore. At this rate, there'll be no sacrificial animals to offer by Passover.

Philip: Look out for the goats!

Approaching the dove sellers, He shouted,

Jesus: *Get these out.*
Don't turn My Father's house to a market!

He went to the forex traders and flipped their tables, spilling coins of various denominations to the ground.

Philip: Hi, Andrew! Hi Simon! You came early too.

Andrew: Hey! What's going on? Isn't that Jesus?

Philip: Yes. I'm amazed how no one has arrested Him yet. What are you doing here? Where's your master?

Andrew: Johannes? He's in Herod's court. Herod summoned him for some reason.

Jesus flips another table.

Simon (Peter): Yikes! Isn't He your Master?
Aren't you going to stop Him?

Nathanael: No. All this makes sense.
Remember what was written?

"Zeal to God's house will consume Me."

-psalter

Philip: Speaking of arrest, look!

Some Jews got together and confronted Jesus.

Jehubed: What are You doing?
Who gave You the right to do this?

Shaal: Hold on. I think I've seen Him.
He's the One the Baptist called,
"Lamb of God."

Jehubed: What "Lamb of God"?
You mean Abraham's . . .

Shaal: Yes, but Johannes can't be right. How can a person be the lamb? That's why everyone thinks Johannes is a fraud!

Jehubed: Hey! If You are a prophet,
then show us a sign from God
that You are authorised to do this.

107

Jesus:	*Here's a sign: Destroy this Temple,* *and in three days, I will raise it up.*
Jehubed:	What?! You can't rebuild it in three days. It took 46 years to build this.

Thing is, when Jesus said, "this Temple," He was referring to His body. His disciples remembered this scene and what He said after He was raised from the dead. Although they did not know what was going on this time, this will later help them believe what Jesus and the Scriptures said.

Meanwhile, in Herod's Court   32
(Mk 6:17b–20a)

Location Stamp   : Herod's Palace, Jerusalem

Approaching the throne room, Herodias overhears a lecture from a familiar voice. The voice seems to be aimed at her husband and king. She started teasing Herod as she turned towards the throne.

Herodias:	My dear, who is lecturing you about what to do and not to . . . Johannes! Herod, why is he here? Again!
Herod:	Dear, I invited him over so we can hear a holy and righteous man's thoughts on the Passover.
Johannes:	It is illegal for you to have your brother's wife.

He enjoys listening to Johannes even though listening to him makes him doubt his own decisions.

Herodias:	How dare you? Guards! Kill this man!
Herod:	Halt! It is not right to kill our guest after they have responded to our invitation.
Herodias:	Why are you protecting him?
Herod:	I invited him as a guest. Please!
Herodias:	I don't care who he is. I want him dead!
Herod:	Johannes, please excuse us. Until next time!

After Johannes left the courtroom . . .

Herodias:	I will have him arrested, you hear me? There's nothing you can do that can stop me!
Herod:	You will not cause an outrage at this time of the year. Everyone thinks he is a prophet. Do you want the people to riot before Passover? We don't want a repeat of the first Passover when I first became king.
Herodias:	What if I arrest my enemy after the holy days? Will my king stop me?
Herod:	You have my word.

What to do in Jerusalem?   33
(Jn 2:23–25)

People saw what Jesus did in Jerusalem on that Passover celebration, and many believed in His name. However, Jesus did not entrust

Himself to them. He did not need anyone's introduction because He knows what was in every person's heart.

Jehubed:	How dare that Man! Who does He think He is?
Nicodemus:	Calm down. What's going on?
Jehubed:	That upstart dared to reject my invitation to eat at my place.
Shaal:	Of course, He'll turn you down. A minute before you invited Him, you were ready to beat Him up.
Jehubed:	Who wouldn't? Just because that prophet said He's the Lamb of God, He now thinks He is a big shot. Do you know what He did at the temple earlier?
Nicodemus:	I did. Hold on, did you say Lamb? As in, "Lamb of God"?
Shaal:	Remember when we went out to investigate Johannes?
Nicodemus:	The Baptist, yes.
Shaal:	Apparently, he identified Jesus as the Lamb of God.
Nicodemus:	Jesus who?
Shaal:	Jesus bar Joseph, the Nazarene.
Nicodemus:	I know Him! I heard that He did something unbelievable in Cana when I attended that wedding.

Shaal:	He was there? Shikor told me something about the best wine in Cana but he didn't tell me anything about Jesus.
Nicodemus:	Tell me more about your report on Johannes. I just might pay this Jesus a visit soon.
Jehubed:	Take me when you go. I want to see His face when you expose that fraud!
Nicodemus:	If I take you, I'll be barred at His door. Hahaha!
Jehubed:	I don't care! I want to see Him realise how wrong He is to think we are cheating people!

From Jerusalem to Galilee

Born Again: How and Why – Eternal Life #1   34
(Jn 3:1–21)

Time Stamp   : 24 April AD 31
Location Stamp   : Some inn in Jerusalem

Knocking at the inn door, we find Nicodemus shaking off his companion.

Shaal:	They just finished supper. It's unusual to receive a visitor at this time.
Nicodemus:	Don't worry about it. This happens all the time.
John:	Good evening. Yes, who is . . . Nicodemus! Sir! What brings you here?

Nicodemus:	John! I came to pay the Rabbi a visit.
John:	You mean, Jesus? Yes, He's in. Have you had supper?
Nicodemus:	It's all right, I just finished mine too. I came here for a nice evening chat with the Rabbi.
John:	Please come in.
Nicodemus:	It's just me. My friend walked me here but he's in a hurry. Thank you for accompanying me, Shaal. Take care!
Shaal:	Why . . .
Nicodemus:	Bye!

Inside, John introduced the Pharisee to Jesus and had them seated.

Nicodemus:	Rabbi, we know that God sent You to teach because no one can do what You did if God wasn't with You.

Now, Johannes talked about how near the Kingdom is. If he is correct, when is it coming?

Jesus:	*Truth is you cannot see the Kingdom of Heaven unless you're born from above.*
Nicodemus:	Born?! How can an old man like me return to my mother's womb and be born again?

Jesus: *But it is, I assure you!*
You must be born of water and the Spirit
to enter the Kingdom of God.

Those born from a human is human,
but those born from the Holy Spirit is spirit.

So, don't be too surprised when I say,
"You must be born from above."

Nicodemus: *stomped*

Jesus: *It's like the wind,*
it blows when and where it wants.
You can hear it,
but you can't tell where it came from
or where it's going.

The same is true for those born of the Spirit.

Nicodemus: How is this even possible?

Jesus: *You're a teacher of Israel.*
How come you don't know this?

Look,
We tell others what We know
and certify what We have seen.
But you refuse to accept what We say.

If you don't believe Me
when I talk about things on earth,
then how are you going to believe
when I talk about things in heaven?

Nicodemus: Can I go up to heaven to confirm this?

Jesus: *No one can go up to heaven*
              except the Son of man
              Who came down from heaven.

Nicodemus: No one can rest in the bosom of Abraham until
              they die. When that happens, there's no coming
              back to tell others what's on the other side.

Jesus: *Unless they have eternal life.*

Nicodemus: How can anyone have eternal life?

Jesus: *Remember what happened*
              when Moses lifted the snake in the desert?

Nicodemus: They were saved from certain death.

Jesus: *In the same way,*
              the Son of Man must be lifted
              so everyone who believes in Him
              will have eternal life.

Nicodemus: Who is this Son of Man?
              Is this the same man that Daniel mentioned?

Jesus: *He is God's only Son.*

Nicodemus: If He is God's Son,
              shouldn't He be in heaven?

Jesus: *God loves the world so much*
              that He gave it His only Son.

Nicodemus: Why would God give His Son to the world?

Jesus: *To give the world eternal life.*

Nicodemus: How can the world
get eternal life from His Son?

Jesus: *By believing in the Son of Man,*
they will not die,
they will have eternal life.

Nicodemus: Is this a new teaching? Because every time the Scripture talks about God's plan for the world, it talks about judgement, specifically judgement day. Was the Son sent to finally bring God's judgement to the world?

Jesus: *God did not send His Son*
to judge the world.
God sent His Son
to save the world through Him.

In fact,
there is no judgement
against anyone who believes Him.
But anyone who does not believe Him
is already judged
for not believing
in the Name of God's only Son.

Nicodemus: We are judged
for not believing in His Son's name?
How is that the basis?

Jesus: *This is the basis:*
            Light came to the world,
            but people loved darkness over Light
            because of their evil acts.

Nicodemus: How do we know if people are evil?

Jesus: *Everyone who commits evil*
            hates the Light.
            They refuse to go to the Light
            to keep their actions in secret.

            However,
            those who commit the truth
            bask in the Light,
            revealing God's work.

Nicodemus: Speaking of the truth, don't you think it is normal
            for the temple shekel to have greater value than
            Roman coins?

The night continued with everyone joining in the conversation.

"Jesus, because…" ~ Herald   35
(Jn 3:22–36; Mt 14:5; Jn 4:2)

Time Stamp   : 25 April to 2 May AD 31
Indicative Event(s) : Passover & Feast of Unleavened Bread passed

Time Stamp   : 3 May AD 31
Location Stamp   : Herod's Court, Jerusalem

Herod: What's going on?

Herodias: The holy days are over.

Herod:	What does that have to do with this squad?
Herodias:	You promised me!
Herod:	Which one?
Herodias:	Are you playing dumb or do you really have no plans to get rid of my enemies?
Herod:	Which enemy?
Herodias:	Johannes! You said you'll kill him after the Passover!
Herod:	Oh that . . .
Herodias:	Don't "oh that" me! Captain! Go ahead and kill that man. He should be somewhere near the river.
Herod:	Captain, arrest that man and have him imprisoned. We will not kill an innocent man.
Herodias:	I want him dead!
Herod:	I know, but we can't kill a prophet. The people will mob us!
Chayal:	My lord, on what charges shall we arrest him if he's innocent?
Herodias:	What are you saying? Soldiers arrest people! If they resist, show them your fist! If they open their mouth, shut it with your feet! If they . . .

Herod sighs as he shook his head and sighed over the sound of his wife's motivating speech.

Location Stamp   : Somewhere outside Jerusalem within Judea

Jesus and His disciples left Jerusalem and went to the land of Judea. Jesus spent time with His disciples there, where they started baptising people.

Location Stamp   : Aenon near Salim

People still go out of their way to get baptised by Johannes. So, he washed them at the waters near Salim, where there is plenty of water. That time, Johannes' disciples got into a quarrel with Jews regarding purification.

Bea: If your master already found the Man he was looking for, then why are you still here?

Andrew: Were you paying attention? Finding the Baptiser of the Holy Spirit is not his only mission but He is also here to prepare the way of the Lord.

Shaal: Then why are you still baptising people?

Kittaw: Who else will do it?
                He is the prophet of our times!

Shaal: In case you missed it,
                Jesus is also out baptising.

Kittaw: Jesus who? What do you mean?

Bea: You don't know? Jesus of Nazareth and His growing number of disciples are baptising people not far from here.

Andrew: ??

John: Come, let's check out what these haters are talking about and prove to them that our master is the only Baptiser in town.

A few hours' walk away, they found the disciples of Jesus baptising people.

John: Philip, what are you guys doing?

Philip: Weren't you there when Jesus was talking to Nicodemus? People must be born of the water and the Spirit.

John: Yes, but . . .

Andrew: What is he talking about?

John explained to Andrew the conversation between Jesus and Nicodemus. When they got back to the Baptist, they reported what they saw.

Kittaw: Teacher, do you remember the One you baptised in the river? The One you called, "Lamb of God"?

Johannes: Jesus, the One who will baptise with the Holy Spirit? Yes, why?

Kittaw: The Jews said He is also baptising people and we did see them doing it. Now everybody goes to Him instead of us.

Johannes: Look,
no one receives anything
unless it is given from heaven.

119

John: But . . .

Johannes: You do remember me saying,
            "I am not the Messiah,"
            and that I was sent
            to prepare the way for Him.

            It is the groom who marries the bride.
            The best man's joy is to stand with Him
            and hear His vows

            This makes me happy.
            He is meant to become greater
            as I fizzle out.

            One who comes from above
            is greater than all.
            One who came from earth
            is from the earth
            and talks about earth.

            One who came from heaven
            is greater than all.
            He talks about everything
            He has seen and heard.
            Too bad, no one believes Him.

            Everyone who accepts His testimony
            certifies that God is real.

Kittaw: How does believing
            Jesus confirm that God is real?

Johannes: Those sent by God
            speak God's words.

Kittaw: How does Jesus do that?

Johannes: Unlike God's servants in the past,
            God gave Jesus the Spirit without limit.

Kittaw: Why would God do that?

Johannes: The Father loves His Son, that's why.
            Also, He placed everything into His hands.
            Everyone who believes in God's Son
            has eternal life.
            Others who do not obey the Son
            will never find life.
            They stay in the queue of God's wrath.

Stop the Herald   36
(Lk 3:19–20; Mk 6:17a; Mt 14:3–4)

Chayal: Everyone, get out of the way! *seized Johannes*
            You are coming with us.

Kittaw: What are you doing?
            Where are you taking our master?

Chayal: This is none of your business!
            fist to the face

Kittaw: I remember you! You were baptised by our
            master! What happened to you?

Chayal: If you will not get out of our way, my spear will
            gut you all until your blood colours the Dead Sea!

After a short struggle, Johannes was bound and taken away. With
this, Herod added the imprisonment of Johannes' to his evil deeds.

Man on a Mission   37
(Mk 1:14a; Mt 4:12; Jn 4:1, 3)

Location Stamp   : Somewhere outside Jerusalem

Philip: Kittaw, what happened to you?

Nathanael: Come here, let me tend to your wounds.

John: We need to see my cousin.

Philip: I'll call Him over. First, relax and tell us what
               happened. Start from the top.

Kittaw told them about the argument they had with the Pharisees
and what happened when they got back and reported to Johannes.

Kittaw: Lord, your cousin Johannes was arrested by
               Herod's men!

Philip: What now, John?
               What are you planning to do?

John: You know what happens when a rabbi dismisses
               his initiates.

Philip: Aiyoo! Even if you have the potential to become
               the Baruch of today's Jeremiah, there's no
               teaching or learning anything when your master is
               in prison. Is Kittaw the only one who was hurt?

Kittaw: A few of us fought back but the master
               surrendered himself. They bound him and then .
               . . *sob*

Philip:	Now, now!

Nathanael:	Lord, it might not be safe to stay near Jerusalem. Herod's palace is not far from here. You could be next.

Jesus:	*We'll be heading to Galilee.*

Nathanael:	But, Lord, that is Herod's domain!

Jesus:	*The Kingdom of God is near!*

Philip:	!!

Nathanael:	!!

John:	!!

"I thirst" ~ Jesus   38
(Jn 4:4–38, 44)

Time Stamp   : 4 May AD 31
Location Stamp   : Jacob's Well, Sychar, Samaria

From Judea, Jesus and His disciples travelled through Samaria until they reached the field that Jacob gave to his son Joseph. Tired from Their journey, Jesus sat by the well.

John:	And that's when Andrew decided to head back to Bethsaida with Simon.

Philip:	He must've been heartbroken.

Nathanael:	We can stop here before we enter Galilee.

Philip:	Lord, You can stay here while we buy food.
Nathanael:	The village market should be open at this time, come!
John:	Auntie, would you like to come with us?
Mary:	Yes, please.

Time Stamp   : 12:00 n.n.

A Samaritan woman came to draw water.

Jesus:	*Give Me a drink.*
Photina:	Excuse me? Why are you asking me for a drink? In case you missed it, You are a Jew, and I am a Samaritan woman.
Jesus:	*If you only knew Who asked you for a drink* *and the gift God has for you,* *you'd be the one asking* *and He would give you Living Water.*
Photina:	Lord, fact check: This well is deep. You don't have anything. Where would you get this living water? You're not greater than our father, Jacob, who gave us this well?
Jesus:	Jacob . . .

Photina:	Yes, Jacob, OUR ancestor. He himself drank here. Him, his children, and his livestock.
Jesus:	*Everyone who drinks the water here* *will be thirsty again.* *But whoever drinks the Water I give* *will never thirst again.* *This Living Water* *turns to a spring inside them* *giving eternal life.*
Photina:	I won't be thirsty again? That means I won't ever have to come here to get water . . . Lord, please give me this water!
Jesus:	*First, go get your husband.*
Photina:	Oh, but . . . I don't have a husband.
Jesus:	*You are correct* *even though you actually had five husbands.* *It is also true* *that you're not married* *to the man you're with.*
Photina:	How did You . . .? Are You a prophet? If You are, then tell me why do you Jews insist that Jerusalem is the only place to worship, when

even our ancestors have been worshipping on this mountain forever?

Jesus: *Woman, believe Me,*
                  the time is coming when
                  you will neither worship the Father
                  in this mountain nor Jerusalem.

                  You Samaritans worship what you don't know
                  but we Jews worship what we know.
                  This is why salvation comes through the Jews.

                  Don't worry, the time is coming.
                  In fact, the time is now!

The disciples of Jesus returned and wondered why He's talking to a woman, but none of them dared ask what's going on.

Jesus: *Now is the time*
                  when true worshipers
                  will worship the Father
                  in spirit and in truth.

                  The Father actively searches
                  for those who worship Him this way.

Photina: Why?

Jesus: *Because God is Spirit.*

                  It then follows that those who worship Him
                  must worship in spirit and in truth.

126

Photina:	This stuff that You're saying is deep. Too deep.
	I know the Messiah, the One called Christ, is coming. When He comes, He will explain everything to us.
Jesus:	*That'd be Me.*
Photina:	You?! Whu . . . Are You . . . Wait! Wait! Wait here!

The woman ran back to the village
and left her jar beside the well.

Philip:	Rabbi, we bought some food. Here, eat something.
Jesus:	*I had food you do not know of.*
Philip:	Did someone bring Him food while we were gone?
Nathanael:	Maybe the woman did.
John:	Nah, maybe an angel!
Jesus:	*My nourishment comes from doing the will of God, who sent Me, and from finishing His work.*
Nathanael:	What does God want us to do?

Jesus:	*After planting, don't they say,* *"We'll harvest in four months"?*
Philip:	Harvest? What are we harvesting?
Jesus:	*Open your eyes and look.* *The fields are ripe and ready for harvest.*
John:	What do we get for harvesting God's field?
Jesus:	*Harvesters are paid well.* *Those who reap will gather eternal life.*
Philip:	Where is this field, and who planted it?
Nathanael:	Does it matter who did the planting?
Jesus:	*Exactly! That's why* *I'm sending you to harvest what you didn't plant* *so those who reap can share the joy of the sowers!*
Philip:	So when are we going to meet these planters?
Jesus:	*You know the adage,* *"One plants and another harvests"?* *Their work is completed.* *Now it's your turn to harvest.*

One Luminous Points to the Light   39
(Jn 4:39–43)

Location Stamp   : Jacob's Well, Samaria

Photina:	Come! There's a Man at the well who told me everything I ever did!
Emet:	Is that possible? How could He possibly know your life story?
Photina:	He said He is the Messiah! He just might be the One?
Shemai:	I met a traveller from Jerusalem last week. He said a guy named Joshua made a scene there.
Hoshama:	Yeah, I heard about it too. The Guy trashed their temple. It must be Him.
Shemai:	Come, everyone! If He is the Messiah, then He must have come to restore our heritage.
Hoshama:	Down with the Jews! Let's go!
Janai:	What's the fuzz about? What did you just say about the Messiah?
Emet:	I don't know but I wanna see. Come!
Janai:	Hold on! Is the Messiah really outside?
Emet:	I don't know, but Photina said He knew everything. Only God can do that!

The people who heard her in the streets came streaming from the village to see Him. Many who saw the commotion went out and followed the crowd.

Emet: Please come and stay here in our village.

Jesus stayed for two days and left on the first day after the Sabbath.

Time Stamp   : Rishon/Sunday, 6 May AD 31

Philip: Farewell, everyone the Lord needs to continue His ministry and preach in Galilee.

Emet: The Lord bless You all and keep you safe in your journey.

Photina: Do you believe me now? How could anyone know everything I ever did?

Shemai: I believe Him now.

Hoshama: I believe Him too, not just because of what you told us.

Shemai: I heard everything He said.
I believe He is the Messiah.

Janai: The promised Messiah is here!
He will save Samaria!

Emet: This Man is not just the Saviour of Samaria, He is the Saviour of the world!

First Missionary Tour: Galilee

Overview
(Jn 4:45; Lk 4:14–15a; Mk 1:14b–15; Mt 4:13b–17)

Jesus continued His journey to Galilee filled with the power of the Holy Spirit. The Galileans welcomed Him because they were in Jerusalem at Passover where they saw everything He did.

His first stop was Nazareth. From there, He found a place to stay in Capernaum, beside the Sea of Galilee. This region is the ancient land assigned to the tribe of Zebulun and Naphtali. This fulfilled what God said through His prophet,

Isaiah: *In the land of Zebulun and Naphtali,*
            beside the sea beyond the Jordan River,
            in Galilee, where foreigners stay,
            people who sat in darkness saw a great light.
            Light dawned to them who lived
            in the shadow of death.

There, He and His two disciples announced God's Good News.

Jesus: *At last! The time promised by God is here!*
            Repent and believe the Good News
            for the Kingdom of God is near!

Reports about Jesus quickly spread throughout Galilee where He taught in their synagogues.

Rejected at Nazareth #1: Debut   40
(Lk 4:16–30)

Time Stamp   : 8 May AD 31
Location Stamp : Nazareth, Galilee

From Sychar, Samaria, Jesus reached Nazareth, Galilee, the town where He grew up.

131

Passover #1

Time Stamp : Sabbath, 12 May AD 31
Location Stamp : Synagogue in Nazareth, Galilee

Jesus always went to the synagogue on Sabbath, even at the beginning of His ministry. On His first public teaching, He took His place and stood up to read. They handed Him the scroll of the prophet Isaiah. He looked for a particular passage in the scroll then read.

Jesus:

The Lord's Spirit is upon Me
because He empowered Me
to announce the Good News
to those in fetal position.

He sent Me
to heal those whose hearts are crushed,
to release the captives,
to give sight back to the blind,
to set the oppressed free,
and to announce the Lord's jubilee.

~ Isaiah

He rolled up the scroll, passed it to the attendant, and sat. All eyes were locked on to Him.

Jesus: *What you heard Me read is fulfilled today!*

Everyone who heard His gracious words wondered,

<u>A</u>beiron: Did He just claim to be the Chosen One?

132

Korach:	Clearly, He is good at the Scriptures, but isn't He Joseph's son?
Datan:	Yes, Joseph the carpenter. I don't remember either of them under the yoke of any prominent rabban.
Abeiron:	Nor any rabbi!
Korach:	So how can He be the Messiah?
Jesus:	*One day you will quote Me on this:* *"Cure yourself, doctor,"* *which means,* *"Do everything You did in Capernaum* *here in Your hometown"*
Datan:	Who do you think You are?
Abeiron:	To us, you're just a carpenter's son!
Korach:	We don't care whatever You're planning to do in Capernaum or anywhere else.
Jesus:	*Correct! No prophet is accepted* *in their hometown.*
Korach:	You did one thing in Jerusalem and now You talk here like some big shot.
Datan:	He actually thinks He's a prophet!
Jesus:	*Remember, in Prophet Elijah's time,* *when heaven was closed and*

a terrible famine hit the land
for three and a half years?

There were many needy widows in Israel,
but Elijah was not sent to them.
Instead, he was sent to Zarephath,
a widow in Sidon.

Same thing during Prophet Elisha's time.
There were many lepers in Israel,
but the only one healed
was a Syrian named Naaman.

Korach: Are you saying we are rejecting a prophet?

Datan: You're not even a prophet! We know You! Mary, what have you been feeding your Son? Stop it!

Korach: You're not special,
              You're just a carpenter's son!

Abeiron: Who are You to tell us,
              "we don't deserve God's help"?

Infuriated, the whole synagogue mobbed Him out of town to the edge of the hill to kick Him out, but He simply cut through the crowd and left.

Philip: Lord, where shall we stay?

Nathanael: You don't need to ask Him that. You know it's still Sabbath, let's camp for now and head out after sunset.

Long Distance Healing #1

(Mt 4:13a; Jn 4:46–54)

"Am I God? Can I give and take life?"

~ Jehoram, King of Israel
(2 Kings 5:7bc)

Time Stamp   : Rishon, 13 May AD 31
Location Stamp   : Cana, Galilee

From Nazareth, Jesus passed by Cana on His way to Capernaum. This is where Jesus will perform His second miraculous sign. This also where He turned water into wine.

Time Stamp   : 14 May AD 31
Location Stamp   : Capernaum, Galilee

Hermogenes: Master, I have news for you.

Samlah: Yes, what is it?

Hermogenes: Do you remember the Man who they said turned water into wine?

Samlah: The Son of Joseph? Yes, why?

Hermogenes: One of the merchants just arrived and reported that He's back in Cana. Maybe He can do a miracle for your son.

Samlah: How do we know He's still there? When did the merchant leave Cana?

Hermogenes:	He left Cana yesterday. I'm not sure if the Son of Joseph is still in . . .
Samlah:	Hurry, saddle the fastest horses and come with me.

Time Stamp   : A little before 1:00 p.m.
Location Stamp : Cana, Galilee

Philip:	Lord, an official arrived from Capernaum looking for You. He seems to know You from Cana.
Samlah:	Lord, I pray You can still remember me from the wedding two months ago. I remembered how You turned water into wine. Now I have a son in Capernaum who is dying. Perhaps You can heal my son.
Jesus:	*If you people do not see signs and wonders you never believe.*
Samlah:	Lord, I beg You. Please come with us now before my son dies.
Jesus:	*Go, your son lives.*

Time Stamp   : 15 May AD 31
Location Stamp : Road to Capernaum, Galilee

Hermogenes:	Master, what do we do now? He did not come with us.
Samlah:	He said my son lives. That's all we need to hear. Remember what Naaman's servants said?

Hermogenes: Yes, if a prophet said so . . . look, master! That looks like one of your servants. Hey, Charmion! Come! It's us!

Samlah: Charmion, is everything alright? What brings you here?

Charmion: Master, your son is alive!

Samlah: Praise the Living God!

Hermogenes: How did you know? What happened?

Charmion: His fever broke yesterday and before we knew it, he has completely recovered.

Samlah: What time did he recover?

Charmion: Yesterday afternoon at one o'clock.

Hermogenes: Master! It was one o' clock when the Lord said, *"Your son lives"*!

He reached home and told his entire household what happened, and they all believed in Jesus.

Part 2: First Disciples 42
(Mk 1:16–20; Mt 4:18–22; Lk 5:1–11)

Time Stamp : 16 May AD 31
Location Stamp : Capernaum, Galilee

From Cana, Jesus headed to Capernaum.

John:	Cousin, we're off.
Philip:	Where are you going?
John:	Our rabbi has told us to return to our trades. *choked* I'm going back to join James and my father.
Nathanael:	We'll see you around.
John:	Take care, Auntie.
Mary:	Send my greetings to Salome.

Time Stamp   : 18 May AD 31
Location Stamp : Gennesaret, Sea of Galilee

As Jesus was walking along the shores of the Sea of Galilee, He saw Simon, (the one He called Peter on their first meeting,) and His brother Andrew throwing their net into the water. They were washing it because they were fishermen before they became disciples of Johannes. Now that Johannes is imprisoned, they went back to fishing.

He started preaching and a crowd gathered to listen to God's words.

Nathanael:	Lord, there's too many people. You'll be forced into the water if we don't do something about it.
Philip:	Look! There are two boats here. How about standing on one of them as we keep people on dry land.
Jesus:	*Is this your boat?*

Simon (Peter): Yes, Lord.

Jesus: *Do you mind pushing it out a bit*
so I can teach from your vessel?

Simon (Peter): Give me a minute.

Jesus stepped into the boat, and Simon obliged. Sitting at the boat, He taught the crowds.

After the crowds were dismissed . . .

Jesus: *Let's go to deeper waters.*
Out there, drop your nets
and catch some fish.

Simon (Peter): Master, we all worked hard last night
and caught nothing.
But if You say so,
we'll give it one more shot.

They took their boats to the deep, where they cast their nets. This time they caught such a huge haul that their nets began to tear! James and John, the sons of Zebedee, were fishing nearby when they heard their shout for help. The catch was so big that both boats were on the verge of sinking. Simon, Andrew, James, John, and everyone who helped were in awe of what just happened. Simon fell to his knees in front of Jesus.

Simon (Peter): Lord, please leave me, for I am a sinner.

Jesus: *Don't be afraid!*
From now on, you will be catching people!

Come, follow Me. I will show you how.

As soon as they landed, Simon and Andrew left their nets, the catch, everything, and followed Jesus.

James and John, whose boats were docked farther up the shore with their father Zebedee and their hired men were repairing their nets when Jesus saw them.

Zebedee:	This is a huge catch! Keep this up and you'll be good for life.
John:	I think this is only possible because Jesus was there.
Zebedee:	Your cousin Jesus went with you fishing?
John:	No, He was in Simon's boat when they caught the huge haul.
Zebedee:	Well, this is a miraculous catch. I don't remember James catching this much too. Much less I!
James:	Look, there He is!
John:	Greetings, cousin . . .
Jesus:	*Come! Follow Me!*
James:	!!
John:	!!
Zebedee:	Well? I know you both want this. Go!

At once, they too followed Him, leaving Zebedee in the boat with the hired men.

Who is the Boss?   43
(Mk 1:21–28; Lk 4:31–37)

Time Stamp   : Later the same day
Location Stamp   : Capernaum, Galilee

Mary: Son, supper is almost . . . John?

John: Yes, it's me, Auntie!

Mary: I know, but what are you all doing here?

John: Our Rabbi has called us!

Mary: Wow! Praise God!

John: Look! James, Andrew, and Simon too.

Mary: You can tell me later what happened over supper.

Nathanael: Please, allow us to help . . .

James: Auntie, have you decided to stay here?

Time Stamp   : Sabbath, 19 May AD 31
Location Stamp   : Synagogue in Capernaum, Galilee

Jesus went to the synagogue and taught the people. People were blown away because He taught with authority unlike teachers of religious law. Suddenly, a man possessed by a demon started shouting,

Possessed: Ha! What do You want from us,
                Jesus of Nazareth?
                Have You come to destroy us?

> I know who You are,
> You are God's Holy One!

Jesus: *Silence! Get out of Him.*

The demon threw the man to a convulsion before coming out with a wail. The man was left on the ground unharmed. Everyone was blown away.

Manna: What's this?

Aspasia: His teachings are new.

Manna: And authoritative!

Onan: His words even have power to make evil spirits leave.

The news about Jesus quickly spread to throughout Galilee.

Hermogenes: Master, Jesus is in town. He was seen earlier at the synagogue and exorcised one guy.

Samlah: Quick, tell the others.
Tell everyone who needs someone healed.

Everything happens on Rishon/Sunday   44
(Mt 8:14–17; Mk 1:29–34; Lk 4:38–41)

Time Stamp   : Sabbath, 19 May AD 31
Location Stamp : Still in Capernaum, Galilee

From the synagogue,

Philip:	Why did Andrew and Simon leave in a hurry?
John:	Simon's mother-in-law is sick.
Nathanael:	The Lord has healed an official's son before. Ask Him.
John:	Lord, please come. We know You are capable of healing.
James:	She stays with Simon, and their house is nearby. Come, Lord, we'll show you where.

At Simon's house . . .

Andrew:	Lord, please come in. We're sorry we can't welcome you properly. The lady of the house is sick.
John:	Nathanael said that the Lord has once healed a child here in Capernaum.
Simon (Peter):	Lord, please come and heal her too. She is sick in bed.

Jesus stood at her bedside, rebuked the fever, then took her by the hand, and the fever left her. He helped her up, and she went to serve them.

Time Stamp   : after 6:00 p.m., Rishon/Sunday, 19 May AD 31

That evening, after sunset, people throughout the village brought their sick friends and relatives, including demon-possessed people, to Jesus. The whole town gathered at the door watching when . . .

Possessed #2: You! You are the Son of G . . .

Jesus: *Out!*

All spirits were exorcised with one word. He did not allow demons to speak because they knew He was the Christ. It was a sight that blew away everyone. He then proceeded to heal various diseases with the touch of His hand.

This fulfilled God's word through His prophet.

Isaiah:

"He took our sicknesses and removed our diseases."

Kingdom of God Tour   45
(Mk 1:35–39; Lk 4:42–43; Mt 4:23–24)

Time Stamp   : Rishon/Sunday, 20 May AD 31
Location Stamp   : Still in Capernaum, Galilee

Before daybreak, Jesus got up, went to an isolated place, and prayed. Simon and the others went out to look for Him.

Simon (Peter): Lord, You're here!
                We've been looking all over for you.

Andrew: When the sun came up, people were already at our door. We told them You already left.

Philip: That was when they came to our place.

John: Someone must have thought You have gone out to some other town.

Simon (Peter): Now, people are begging You to stay.

Jesus: *I must go to other towns too.*
I need to announce the Good News
of the Kingdom of God,
for this is My mission.

Jesus toured the region of Galilee and the rest of the country. He preached in their synagogues, announced the Good News of the Kingdom, healed all kinds of disease and illness, and exorcised demons.

News about Him even reached Syria. Soon, people started bringing Him all who were sick of various diseases, those who suffer in pain and those possessed by demons, epileptics, including paralytics. He healed them all.

Eager to Heal   46
(Mt 4:25; Lk 4:44, 10:38a; Mk 1:40–45; Mt 8:1–4; Lk 4:15b, 5:12–16)

Time Stamp   : 27 May AD 31
Location Stamp   : Bethany, Judea

"Am I God? Why did he send me
someone to be cured of leprosy?"

~ Jehoram, King of Israel
(2 Kings 5:7bd)

Large crowds followed Jesus from Galilee, Decapolis, Jerusalem, Judea, even people from east of the Jordan River. After preaching in one of the synagogues of Judea, He met Martha. On His way down the Mount of Olives, a man covered with leprosy saw Him. The man approached, begged on his knees, then worshipped Him with his face to the ground.

145

Lazarus: Lord, if You are willing, make me clean.

Moved with compassion, Jesus reached out and touched him.

Jesus: *I do want you to be clean.*

Instantly, all signs of leprosy all over his body disappeared and he was clean. Jesus sent him on his way with a stern warning

Jesus: *Don't tell anyone what happened. Go to the priest instead and let him examine you. Bring the required offering in the law of Moses for those healed of leprosy. This will publicly prove that you have been cleansed.*

Instead of following the instructions of Jesus, he went around spreading the word, glorifying Him. He told everyone what happened. Because of this, news of His power spread even faster. Large crowds came and surrounded Jesus to hear Him preach, be healed, and they would praise Him. Now He couldn't enter any town publicly. He had to withdraw and stay in secluded places, like the wilderness, where He prays. Even then, people from everywhere kept coming to Him.

Only God Forgives Sins 47
(Mk 2:1–12; Mt 9:1–8; Lk 5:17–26)

Time Stamp : 31 May AD 31
Location Stamp : Possibly Tiberias

Several days later, Jesus climbed into a boat and went back across the lake to Capernaum, His own town.

Time Stamp : 1 June AD 31
Location Stamp : Jesus' house, Capernaum

146

The news that He was back home quickly spread, and soon the house where He stayed was so packed with visitors that there was no more room, even outside the door. The Lord's healing power was strongly with Him.

Jesus was teaching the crowd when four men arrived carrying a paralysed young man on a sleeping mat. They tried to take him inside but couldn't reach Jesus because of the crowd, so they went up the roof, took off some tiles, and dug a hole above the head of Jesus.

He was preaching God's word when the hole opened up. They lowered the man on his mat into the crowd, right down in front of Jesus. Seeing their faith, He said to the man,

Jesus: *Cheer up, My child! Your sins are forgiven.*

Pharisees and teachers of religious law were sitting nearby when Jesus said this. It seemed that these men showed up from every village in Galilee, Judea, Jerusalem, or wherever Jesus is.

Jehumoreh: What is He saying? That is blasphemy!

Iose: Who does He think He is? God?!
Only God can forgive sins!

Immediately, Jesus knew what they were thinking

Jesus: *Why do you entertain*
evil thoughts in your heart?

What is easier to say, "Your sins are forgiven"
or "Stand up, pick up your mat, and walk"?

147

You know what,
I'll prove to you that the Son of Man
has authority on earth to forgive sins.

He turned to the man.

Jesus: *Stand up, pick up your mat, and head home!*

The man jumped up, grabbed his mat, walked out through the stunned onlookers, and went home praising God. The crowd was amazed with a mix of awe, wonder, and fear.

Thaumaz: We have seen amazing things today!

Manna: We've never seen anything like this before!

Aspasia: Praise God for sending
              A Man with great authority!

Part 3: Disciple #7   48
(Mk 2:13–17; Mt 9:9–13; Lk 5:27–32)

Time Stamp   : Rishon/Sunday, 3 June AD 31
Location Stamp : Shores of Capernaum

Later, Jesus left the town, went out to the lakeshore, and taught the crowds that were coming to Him. As He was walking, He saw Levi, a.k.a. Matthew, son of Alphaeus sitting at his tax collector's booth.

Jesus: *Follow Me and be My disciple*

Levi got up, left everything, and followed Him.

Later that night, Levi held a banquet at his place and invited Jesus as the guest of honour. He also invited His disciples, many tax collectors, and other disreputable sinners. A lot of followers of Jesus are made of these people. Again, teachers of religious law who were Pharisees appeared where He was.

Qarob-nāḥāš: Why does your Teacher eat with such scum?

Jesus heard them bitterly interrogating His disciples.

Jesus: *Healthy people don't need a doctor, but the sick do.*
Now go and learn what God meant in Scripture
when He said,

"I WANT YOU TO SHOW MERCY, NOT OFFER SACRIFICES."

You see, I didn't come to call
those who think they are righteous.
I came to call those who know
they are sinners that need to repent.

Closing Words to the First Missionary Tour of Jesus

The ministry of Jesus in Galilee fulfilled what God said through His prophet.

Isaiah: *"In the land of Zebulun and Naphtali,*
in Galilee, beside the sea,
beyond the Jordan River,
where Gentiles live,

149

people who sat in darkness saw a great light.
Light shone on them who lived
in the shadow of death."

Allegation #2: Jesus = Sabbath Breaker

God told Him to   49
(Jn 5:1–15)

Time Stamp   : 16 June AD 31, Sabbath day before Pentecost
Location Stamp : Jerusalem, Judea

A little after the first month of ministering of Jesus in Galilee, He
returned to Jerusalem to observe Pentecost. Inside the city, near the
Sheep Gate, was the pool of Bethesda, with five covered porches.
Crowds of sick people (blind, lame, or paralysed) lay on the porches,
waiting for the water to move in a certain way. This happens when
God's angel comes and stirs the water, but this only happens
occasionally. When the water does finally move, the first person to
step in is sure to be healed of whatever disease they had. One of
those lying there is a man who has been sick for 38 years. It was a
Sabbath (rest day) when Jesus saw him and approached him knowing
He had been ill for a long time.

Jesus:	*Would you like to get well?*
Ra'yasaf:	I can't, sir. I don't have anyone who will put me in the pool when the water bubbles up. Someone else always beats me to it.
Jesus:	*Stand up, pick up your mat, and walk!*

150

The man was instantly healed! He rolled up his sleeping mat and started walking! Jesus was already out of the pool area when Jewish leaders noticed him walking away with his mat.

Laban:	Hold it right there!
Ra'yasaf:	Yes?
Laban:	Have you lost your mind? Have you forgotten it is the Sabbath?
Martin:	You can't work on the Sabbath! The law doesn't allow you to carry that sleeping mat!
Ra'yasaf:	But the Man who healed me told me, *"Pick up your mat and walk."*
Laban:	Who would say such a thing?

The man looked but Jesus is nowhere to be seen.

Ra'yasaf:	He . . . I . . . I don't know where He went.
Laban:	Tell you what, when you see Him, report Him to us. Much better if you can identify Him.
Martin:	You better give the required offering to God. Don't you forget!
Laban:	And drop that mat. You are not allowed to work!

Jesus later found him in the Temple.

Jesus: *Now that you are well, stop sinning or something worse may happen to you.*

Ra'yasaf: You are the One everyone is talking about! You are Jesus!

He went to the Jewish leaders and told them it was Jesus who healed him.

I am, because God does – Eternal Life #3   50
(Jn 5:16–30)

The Jewish leaders went out and looked for Jesus. Once they found Him, they started harassing Him.

Felix: Why did you cause someone to sin?

Laban: Why did you tell someone to work on a Saturday by telling him to carry his mat?

Felix: Are you teaching everyone to break the Sabbath rules?

Jesus: *My Father is always working, and so am I.*

The Jewish leaders were so furious that they looked for ways to punish Him by death!

Felix: We should arrest you and stone you now for telling others to break the Sabbath!

Laban: Can we? He was not the one who broke it.

Hiram: No, but even the master who commands his slave
           to work is guilty of this sin.

Felix: Then we should stone Him now. Everyone heard
           what He said. Besides, we have a witness here.

Laban: We need two witnesses.

Felix: Never mind that we all heard Him claim
           He's the Son of God!

Hiram: We can stone Him here and now for blasphemy.

Laban: You are guilty of blasphemy by the testimony of
           more than two witnesses. We can have You
           stoned here, now.

Felix: More so, You dare say
           God works on the day of rest!

Hiram: You even assert that you are equal to God!?
           You are using God as an excuse to sin!

Jesus: *I tell you the truth,*
           the Son can do nothing by Himself.
           He only does what He sees the Father doing.
           Whatever the Father does, the Son also does.

Laban: And why would God show You
           what He is doing?

Jesus: *The Father loves the Son,*
           and so He shows Him everything He does.
           In fact, He will show His Son

how to do greater deeds
than healing this man.
When that happens,
you will truly be mind-blown.

Felix: What other great deeds can God do?
Other than healing?

Jesus: *You see, just as the Father gives life*
to those He raises from the dead,
so will the Son give life to anyone He wants.
To add, the Father judges no one.
Instead, He already gave the Son
absolute authority to judge!

That way, everyone will honour the Son
the same way they honour the Father.
Anyone who does not honour the Son
is certainly not honouring
the Father who sent Him.

Felix: Everyone should stop listening to you.
You are claiming to be God
by asserting you are God's Son!

Jesus: *I tell you the truth.*
those who listen to My message
and believe in God
who sent Me
have eternal life.

They will never be condemned for their sins.
They already passed from death into life.

I assure you that the time is coming.
Even now, at this moment,
the dead can hear My voice,
the voice of the Son of God.
Those who listen will live.

Felix: Will You never stop blaspheming God?

Laban: Now You're saying You can give life?

Hiram: He's calling Himself our judge too!

Jesus: *The Father has life in Himself, and*
He granted that same life-giving power
to His Son.

He gave Him authority to judge everyone too
because He is the Son of Man.

Hiram: See?!

Laban: We better report Him to the Sadducees. He's now
lecturing us about judgement, and resurrection.

Jesus: *Don't be surprised!*
In time, all the dead in their graves
will hear the voice of God's Son,
then they will rise again.

Those who committed good deeds
will rise to eternal life, and
those who keep doing evil deeds
will rise to be judged.

155

Felix:	Who gave You the authority to judge us?
Hiram:	Yeah, we better get to the root of this. We better identify who is really running this show.
Felix:	Who sent You? Who gave You Your marching orders?
Jesus:	*I can do nothing on My own.* *I judge as God tells Me.* *That means, My judgement is fair* *because I carry out the will* *of the One who sent Me,* *not My own will.*

Credible Witnesses   51
(Jn 5:31–47)

Laban:	You do know Your statements won't hold up in court.
Hiram:	You will need witnesses to back Your claim.
Jesus:	*If I were to testify for Myself,* *My testimony would not be valid.* *But someone else testify about Me.* *Trust Me, everything He says about Me is true.*

The leaders were huddled to themselves talking but, Jesus knew what they were thinking.

Hiram:	Didn't Johannes get arrested for criticising King Herod, his governor?

Laban:	Can Johannes' testimony hold? People call him a prophet. Some even say he's the Messiah.
Felix:	*SMH* This is troublesome, did you know that Johannes calls Him, "the Messiah"?
Hiram:	I was there… a number of times. I was excited when Johannes talked about the Messiah, the Saviour. Too bad I wasn't there when he identified the Messiah.
Laban:	Me too. But this Man can't be the Messiah. He breaks the law and tells everyone to break the Sabbath!
Felix:	This is an isolated case. This is the first time we saw Him order someone to work.
Jesus:	*I know you sent investigators* *to listen to Johannes.* *I assure you his testimony about Me was true.* *Well, I don't need human witnesses,* *but I say these things so you might be saved.* *Johannes was like* *a burning and shining lamp.* *You do admit you were excited* *about his message* *for a while,* *but I have proofs that weigh more* *than the testimony of Johannes'.*
Laban:	What are Your proofs then?

Jesus: *My proofs are My teachings and miracles.*
          The Father gave Me these tasks to do,
          and these deeds prove that He sent Me.

Hiram: God will never corroborate Your nonsense!

Jesus: *The Father who sent Me*
          has testified about Me Himself.
          You've never heard His voice
          nor seen Him face-to-face,
          and His message does not live in you,
          because you do not believe
          in the One He sent to you —
          yes, Me. You do not believe in Me.

Laban: We are God's people, and we have the record of
          God's message. None of it says anything about
          your claims!

Jesus: *You search the Scriptures all your life*
          you think they give you eternal life, but
          you have missed the point.
          The Scriptures point to Me!

          Even so, you still refuse
          to come to Me
          to receive this life.

Hiram: I can't believe
          He is actually claiming to be the Messiah.

Laban: Did the Scripture say anything
          about the Messiah giving life?

Hiram: Quiet! He has just called us people who do not obey God!

Felix: This is unacceptable! He claims credit to all that the Scripture says about the Messiah.

Jesus: *I don't need your acceptance,*
because I know you're not after God's love.

Laban: I think He's another upstart like Johannes.

Hiram: Will you people never stop bringing trouble to our country? We don't need another false prophet.

Laban: . . . Nor another rebel leader!

Jesus: *See?*
I came to you in God's name,
but you rejected Me.
Now if others come in their name,
you accept them.
With open arms!
This is why you can't believe Me:

You seek each other's acceptance.
You don't care about
the only acceptance that matters —
God's acceptance!

Felix: How dare You?
How dare You accuse us of people pleasing!

Hiram:	Your accusations won't hold weight in God's court! We obey God! Everything Moses wrote in the law, we obeyed!
Laban:	We believe in Moses. Why should we believe in You? You have no right to accuse us!
Jesus:	*I will not be the one who will accuse you* *before the Father.* *Moses himself will accuse you!* *Moses, whom you rely on too much,* *will be the one to accuse you.*
Felix:	Big mistake! He's on our side. We follow the laws he gave us.
Jesus:	*If you really believed Moses,* *then you would believe Me!* *You see?* *He wrote about Me!* *But you don't really believe what He wrote.* *If you can't believe Moses,* *how then can you believe Me?*

Spell: "Inappropriate" or "Not Yet"   52
(Mt 9:14–17; Mk 2:18–22; Lk 5:33–39)

Time Stamp   : 26 July AD 31, Fast of Tammuz
Location Stamp   : Not mentioned, possibly Joppa.

One day the disciples of Johannes and the Pharisees were fasting. The people noticed that disciples of Jesus weren't fasting, so they asked the disciples of Johannes what was going on. They, in turn, couldn't explain the behaviour of the companions of Jesus, so they approached Him.

Kittaw: Why don't your disciples fast and pray regularly like us and the Pharisees? Also, why are your disciples always eating and drinking?

Jesus: *Do wedding guests fast*
while celebrating with the Groom?

Everyone: *stomped*

Jesus: *Of course not!*
They can't mourn
while the Groom is with them.
Someday the Groom
will be taken away from them.
Only then will they fast.

Besides, who would patch an old shirt with cloth taken from a new shirt? The new shirt is wasted, plus the patch will shrink, tearing itself away from the old cloth. That leaves you with two spoiled shirts.

In the same way,
no one puts new wine into old wineskins.
The old skins would burst from the pressure,
spilling the wine and ruining the skins.
New wine should be stored in new wineskins
so that both are preserved.

Thing is those who drink old wine
don't seem to want the new wine.
"The old is just fine," so they say.

Merciful Sabbath Boss: My Priests can Eat   53
(Mk 2:23–28; Mt 12:1–8; Lk 6:1–5)

Time Stamp   : 28 July AD 31
Location Stamp   : Possibly Judea (grain fields around Joppa).

One Saturday Jesus walked through some grain fields with His disciples, and some followers. While passing through, His disciples got hungry, so they broke off heads of grain to eat then rubbed off the husks with their hands. Some of His followers who were Pharisees were indignant.

<u>Bar</u> Rishon: Look, your disciples are breaking the law by harvesting on the Sabbath?

Jesus: *Haven't you read the Scriptures?*

     Have you read the part that recorded what David and his companions did when they were hungry?

     He went into the house of God
     and broke the law
     by eating the sacred loaves of bread
     that only the priests are allowed to eat.

     He even gave some to his companions!

     How about the law of Moses?
     Have you read that in the temple,
     priests on duty may work on the Sabbath?

A month after Passover, Jesus again makes a scene in Jerusalem during Pentecost then tours Judea before going back to Galilee

In case you didn't know,
Someone here is way, WAY
greater than the temple!

But if you knew what God meant
when Scripture said,

"I WANT YOU TO SHOW MERCY,
NOT OFFER SACRIFICES,"

then you would not condemn
My innocent disciples

You see,
The Sabbath was made to meet people's needs,
not for people to meet Sabbath requirements.

With these words, you know
the Son of Man is Lord,
even of the Sabbath!

Sabbath Exemption: Good Deed   54
(Mk 3:1–6; Mt 12:9–15a; Lk 6:6–11)

Time Stamp   : 4 August AD 31
Location Stamp   : Possibly Bethel

"Please ask the LORD your God
to restore my hand again!"

~ Jeroboam, King of Israel
(1 Kings 13:6, NLT)

On another Sabbath, Jesus went to their synagogue again. While Jesus was teaching, He noticed a man with a deformed right hand.

His enemies, teachers of the law and Pharisees, watched Him closely. Aware of a healing He made a few Sabbaths ago, they waited for Him to heal the man so they could accuse Him of working on the Sabbath. Later on, their patience ran out, so they finally posted the question.

Laban: Does the law permit a person to work
    by healing on the Sabbath?

Knowing what they are up to, He called the man over.

Jesus: *Come and stand in front of everyone.*

The man walked up. Then Jesus turned to His critics.

Jesus: *Does the law permit us*
    to commit good deeds on the Sabbath,
    or is it a day for doing evil?
    Is this a day to save life
    or to destroy it?

Not knowing the answer, they couldn't reply to Him.

Jesus: *If your sheep fell in a hole on Sabbath,*
    isn't the act of "pulling it out" work?
    Even so, you still would, right?

Their face changed as they realised the truth in the answer they couldn't say out loud.

Jesus: *Now which is more important,*
                                  a person or a sheep?

Hate started to show in the face of the Pharisees because, for the first time, they realised the answer to the question, but they hated Jesus for knowing the answer. Hate turned to rage as their silence embarrassed themselves in front of the crowd. Society's snob experts are shamed in front of the sinful crowd like half-witted fools.

Jesus: *No answers? I'll tell you the answer:*
                                  Yes, the law does permit us
                                  to do good on the Sabbath.

Jesus looked at the faces of all Pharisees who stood up when the interrogation started. His face showed anger and sad frustration at their stubborn hearts. He turned to the man who was visibly embarrassed in the middle of the crowd.

Jesus: *Hold out your hand.*

The man held out his hand, and… it was restored!

The enemies of Jesus stormed out and started planning what to do with Him.

Laban: He was right. I didn't realise it until I heard it. We can do what is right even if it's a Saturday

Br'Sheni: Are you stupid? His logic is flawed. The law is clear. We are not supposed to work on a Sabbath. Good or bad, we're not supposed to work.

Felix: This can't be good. We need to stop Him from teaching others about these lies. You heard about how He told someone to work last week? With the kind of influence, He has, who knows what He'll tell others next?

Br'Sheni: I have friends who work for Herod. Maybe we could get them to help us get rid of Him.

Felix: With Herod's style, this could be the end of Him.

Br'Sheni: Come. I know where they hang out.

The Pharisees called for a meeting to plan out how to kill Jesus. But Jesus knew what they were plotting.

MARK

1	2	3	4
5	6	7	8
9	10	11	12
13	14	15	16

JOHN

1	2	3	4	5	6	7
8	9	10	11	12	13	14
15	16	17	18	19	20	21

MATTHEW

1	2	3	4	5	6	7
8	9	10	11	12	13	14
15	16	17	18	19	20	21
22	23	24	25	26	27	28

LUKE

1	2	3	4	5	6
7	8	9	10	11	12
13	14	15	16	17	18
19	20	21	22	23	24

A chart showing all chapters of each Gospel. The shading indicates the progress of the narrative with respect to each chapter and book. A shading of Luke 1 to 5 means it has been completed at the end of this book's chapter while 6 is partially completed.

Chapter 5

A King and His Kingdom

And we, apostles and other witnesses, have seen His glory,
the glory of the Father's one and only Son.

No one has ever seen God. But Jesus,
the only begotten God in the Father's bosom, revealed Him.

~ John

Prelude to the Sermon

First–Century Pop Star: A Servant?   55
(Mk 3:7–12; Mt 12:15b–21; Lk 6:17–19)

Time Stamp   : Morning of 9 August AD 31
Location Stamp   : Sea of Galilee, possibly the shores of Bethsaida

Jesus and His disciples came down and headed towards the sea. The news about the things He do spread far and wide that huge numbers of people came to see Him. Jesus stood on a large and level area surrounded by His disciples, His many followers, and the crowd. There were people from Galilee, Judea, Jerusalem, Idumea, from east of the Jordan River, and from as far north as the seacoasts of Tyre and Sidon.

Jesus instructed His disciples to have a boat ready so the crowd would not crush Him. Crowds came to hear Him and be healed of their diseases. He has healed so many people such that everyone, especially sick people, eagerly pushed forward to touch Him. Healing power came out of Him, and He healed everyone but warned them not to tell others.

Even those possessed by evil spirits were healed. Jesus sternly commanded the spirits not to reveal who He was, but every time the evil spirits see Him, they would throw their hosts to the ground, shrieking.

Evil Spirits: You are the Son of God!

This fulfilled what God said through His prophet.

Isaiah:

> *"LOOK AT MY SERVANT,*
> *THE ONE I CHOSE.*
> *HE IS MY BELOVED,*
> *ONE WHO PLEASE MY SOUL.*
> *I PUT MY SPIRIT ON HIM,*
> *AND HE PROCLAIMS JUSTICE*
> *TO THE NATIONS.*
>
> *HE WILL NOT QUARREL, SHOUT,*
> *OR RAISE HIS VOICE IN PUBLIC.*
> *HE WILL NOT CRUSH THE WEAK*
> *NOR SNUFF OUT A DYING CANDLE*
>
> *UNTIL HE MAKES JUSTICE WIN*
> *AND UNTIL THE NATIONS*
> *HAVE PUT THEIR HOPE*
> *ON HIS NAME."*

~ God Almighty

Part 4: The 12 Disciples   56
(Mk 3:13–19; Lk 6:12–16)

Time Stamp   : 6:01 p.m., end of Sabbath, 11 August AD 31
Location Stamp   : Mt Meron overlooking the Sea of Galilee

From the sea, Jesus went up a mountain to pray to God all night.

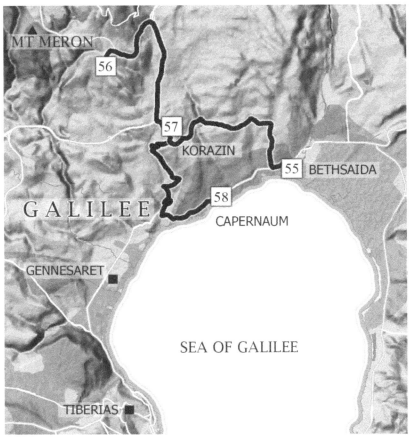

A Prophet like Moses descends the mountain
to appoint leaders and teach the people

Time Stamp   : Rishon/Sunday morning, 12 August AD 31
Location Stamp   : Possibly a level area overlooking Korazin

At daybreak, He called His disciples and they all came. From them, He appointed 12 to accompany Him and gave them authority to exorcise demons. He also called them Apostles because He'll send them out to preach.

172

Here are the names of the twelve:

Simon (whom He named Peter)
James and John (the sons of Zebedee,
but Jesus nicknamed them "Sons of Thunder")
Andrew (Peter's brother)
Philip
Bartholomew, a.k.a., Nathanael
Matthew
Thomas
James (son of Alphaeus)
Thaddaeus (son of James)
Simon (the zealot)
Judas Iscariot (who later betrayed Him).

Sermon at the Mount

The Teacher's Teachings   57
(Mt 5:1–2)

Time Stamp   : Rishon/Sunday afternoon, 12 August AD 31
Location Stamp   : Possibly a level area overlooking Korazin

When He saw the crowd, Jesus went up the hill and sat. His disciples
gathered, and He started to teach them.

Happiness
(Mt 5:3–12; Lk 6:20–23)

He turned to His disciples and said,

A King and His Kingdom

Jesus:

Happy are you who are poor,
you who are poor in spirit,
for God's Kingdom is yours.

Happy are you who are mourning,
for you will be comforted,
and in due time, you will laugh.

Happy are you who are meek
for you will inherit earth.

Happy are you who hunger and thirst
for righteousness,
for you will be filled.

Happy are you who are merciful,
for you will receive mercy.

Happy are you whose hearts are pure,
for you will see God.

Happy are you who make peace,
for you will be called God's children.

Happy are you who are persecuted
for doing what is right,
for the Kingdom of Heaven is yours.

Happy are you when people insult you,
Persecute you,
lie about you,
and say all kind of evil things against you,
because of Me.

Happy are you when people hate you,
exclude you,
insult you,
and call you evil
because of the Son of Man.

When that happens,
be happy!
Be very glad!
Yes, leap for joy!
Look! Great reward awaits you in heaven,
for that is how their ancestors
treated the prophets.

Heads up: Tears
(Lk 6:24–26)

Sorrow awaits you who are rich;
you have received your comfort.

Sorrow awaits you who are full now,
for you will hunger.

Sorrow awaits you who laugh now,
for you will weep and mourn.

Sorrow awaits you who are praised by people,
for this is how their ancestors
treated false prophets.

Salt and Light – Who are We?
(Mt 5:13–16; Lk 11:33)

A King and His Kingdom

You are the salt of the earth.
But if salt becomes useless,
How do you make it salty again?
What will you use it for?

It is good for nothing,
except to throw it out
for people to walk on.

You are the light of the world.
You can't hide a city on a hill.

Nor does anyone light a lamp
and hide it under a basket.
Instead, a lamp is placed on a stand
to shine on everyone home
and those who enter.

In the same way,
let your light shine
for people to see
your good deeds
and glorify your Father
in heaven.

What to do with the Law?
(Mt 5:17–20)

Don't think I came to abolish
the law nor the prophets.
In fact, I came to finish their work.
I tell you the truth,
even after heaven and earth disappears,

none of God's law will disappear
until its purpose is achieved.

So anyone who breaks
the least of these commandments
AND teach others to do the same,
will be called the worst
in the Kingdom of Heaven.

But those who keep the commandments
AND teach others to do the same,
will be called great in the Kingdom of Heaven.

I tell you,
unless your righteousness is greater
than the righteousness
of the scribes and Pharisees,
you will never enter the Kingdom of Heaven.

When to Solve Conflicts
(Mt 5:21–26)

You know how they were told,
"Do not murder" and that
"Whoever murders anyone
will answer to the court"?

I say,
whoever hates their relative
will answer to the court.
Whoever calls their relative useless
will answer to the Church leaders.
Whoever calls anyone fool
will answer to hellfire.

So if you wish to please God
but recall that someone has a case against you,
reschedule your time with God,
get reconciled to that person,
THEN come to serve your God.

On the way to court with your plaintiff,
quickly reach a settlement.
Otherwise, your accuser
will take you to the judge,
who will hand you over to the sheriff
and throw you in prison.

I tell you the truth:
You won't be freed UNTIL
you pay the last penny.

Dealing with Adultery
(Mt 5:27–30)

You heard the saying
"Do not commit adultery."

I say,
whoever looks at others lustfully
already committed adultery.

So if your eye causes you to sin,
gouge it out and throw it away.
It is better for you to lose one part
than for your whole body
to be thrown to hell.

Same thing
if your hand causes you to sin,
cut it off and throw it away.
It is better for you to lose one part
than for your whole body
to be thrown into hell.

Who wins in Divorce?
(Mt 5:31–32)

It is also said that
"Whoever divorces their spouse
must give them a written notice."

I say
everyone who divorces their spouse
for reasons other than sexual immorality
will make them prone to adultery.
Those who marry a divorcée
commits adultery too.

To Vow not to Vow
(Mt 5:33–37)

Remember how they were told
not to swear with fingers crossed.
You must carry out
the vows you make to God.

I say,
do not make vows at all!
Do not promise "by heaven!"
because heaven is God's throne.
Do not promise "by earth!"

179

because earth is God's footstool.
Do not promise "by Jerusalem!"
because Jerusalem is the city of the great King.
Do not promise "by your head"
because you can't change
your hair colour at will.

Just make your,
"Yes" yes
and your
"No" no.
Anything beyond this is from the evil one.

Did Jesus Walk His Talk?
(Mt 5:38–42; Lk 6:29a)

You heard the saying
"An eye for an eye and
a tooth for a tooth."

I say,
do not resist evil!

If someone slaps you on the right cheek,
then offer the other cheek.

If you someone sues you
to take your shirt,
then give it along with your coat.

If you are forced to go one mile,
then go two miles.

180

Give to the one who asks you
and don't turn away
anyone who wants to borrow.

Is Love = Romance?
(Mt 5:43–48; Lk 6:27–36)

You heard the saying,
"Love your neighbours
and hate your enemies."

For those of you who listen to Me, I say,
love your enemies,
pray for your persecutors,
bless those who curse you,
do good to those who hate and persecute you,
and pray for those who mistreat you.

Give to anyone who asks from you.
To those who take what is yours,
do not demand them back.

Do to others what you want them to do to you.

If you love those who love you,
why should you get credit?
Don't sinners do the same?

If you greet only your relatives,
how are you better than anyone else?
Does the world not do the same?

If you do good only to those who do good to you,
why should you get credit?
Even sinners do that!

If you lend only to those who can repay you,
why should you get credit?
Even sinners lend without interest.

Instead,
love your enemies,
do good,
lend without expecting repayment.
THEN
your reward will be great,

and you'll be children
of the Most High God,
your Father in heaven.

For He is kind
to those ungrateful and evil.
He makes His sun rise
on both evil and good
and sends rain
to both righteous and unrighteous.

Therefore, be merciful,
just as your Father in heaven is merciful.
Be perfect,
just as your Father is perfect.

How to Give
(Mt 6:1–4)

Be careful
not to show off your good deeds
to be admired.
If you do,

you will lose your reward
from your Father in heaven.

When you commit an act out of love,
don't announce it publicly
the way hypocrites do
to be praised by people!
I tell you the truth:
Their reward is fully paid.

So
when you commit an act out of love,
don't let your left hand know
what your right hand is doing.

By giving in secret,
your Father, Who sees all secrets,
will reward you.

Prayer (Part 1): Do's and Don'ts
(Mt 6:5–15; Lk 11:1–4)

Time Stamp   : Monday morning, 13 August AD 31

After Jesus prayed, one of His disciples came.

Stephen: Lord, teach us to pray
                  the same way John taught his disciples.

Jesus: *When you pray,*
                  don't pray like hypocrites
                  who love to pray in public
                  where everyone can see.

A King and His Kingdom

I tell you the truth:
Their reward is fully paid.

So
when you pray,
go to your room,
shut your door,
and pray to your Father
who is hidden.

Then your Father,
who sees hidden things,
will reward you.

When you pray,
do not mutter empty words
like pagans.
They think their prayers are heard
because of their eloquence.

So
don't imitate them,
for God, your Father,
knows your needs
way before you ask Him.

So then when you pray, say,

Our Father in heaven,
may Your Name be revered,
may Your Kingdom be established,
may Your will be done
on earth as it is in heaven.

Give us our daily bread each day
and forgive our debts,
the same way we forgive our debtors,
and do not lead us to temptation.
Instead, deliver us from evil

because dominion, power, and glory
belongs to You
forever.
Amen.

If you forgive
other people's mistakes,
your Heavenly Father too
will forgive you.

But if you do not forgive
other people's mistakes,
neither will your Father
forgive your mistakes.

Prayer (Part 2): Attitudes
(Lk 11:5–13; Mt 7:7–11)

Say you went to a friend's house at midnight.

<u>*A*</u>*naideian:*   *Amigo, lend me*
                three loaves of bread.
                My friend just arrived,
                and I have nothing to serve.

<u>*S*</u>*henah:*   *Don't bother me!*
                The door is already locked,

and my kids are all in bed.
I can't get up to help you.

I tell you,
even though they won't get up to help
you for friendship's sake,
they'd still get up to help you
because of your audacity.

And so, I say to you,

ask and you will receive;
seek and you will find;
knock and it shall be opened to you

because
everyone who asks receive,
those who seek find,
and those who knock
are granted access.

Which one of you
will give your child a rock
when they ask for bread?
Or give them a snake
when they ask for fish?
Or give them a scorpion
if they ask for an egg?

If you, evil people, know
how to give good gifts to your children,
how much more will the Heavenly Father
give the Holy Spirit to those who ask Him?

How much more will your heavenly Father
give good things to those who ask Him?

The Golden Rule
(Mt 7:12)

So in everything,
treat others the same way
you want to be treated.
For such is the law.
For such is a prophet.

Fasting: How and Why
(Mt 6:16–18)

Every time you fast,
don't make it obvious.
Hypocrites do this
for people to see.

I tell you the truth:
Their reward is fully paid.

So
when you fast, look fresh
so no one can tell if you are fasting,
except your Father, who is hidden.

Then your Father,
who sees hidden things,
will reward you.

187

How to See the World
(Mt 6:22–23; Lk 11:34–36)

Your eye is the lamp of your body.
When your eye is clear,
your whole body is filled with light.

But when your eye is evil,
your body, is likewise, filled with darkness.

If your body is full of light,
with no dark corners,
then you will shine
as if a spotlight is cast on you.

Make sure that the light in you
is not actually darkness.
If you mistook the darkness in you as light,
how dark is that void!

Are we Priests or Judges?
(Mt 7:1–2; Lk 6:37–38)

Do not judge so you won't be judged.
Do not condemn so you won't be condemned.

Forgive so you will be forgiven.
Give and you will be given
something better in value and quantity.

By your verdict, you will be judged.
The measure you use

to measure others
will be measured on you.

Parable #1: Who is the Teacher? Who to Teach?
(Mt 7:3–6; Lk 6:39–42)

Jesus gave them this parable:

> *The blind cannot lead the blind.*
> *Both will fall into a ditch.*
>
> *Disciples aren't greater than their teacher,*
> *but a fully trained disciple*
> *will become like their teacher.*
>
> *And*
> *why do you look at*
> *the splinter in someone's eye*
> *but not see the shingle in your eye?*
>
> *How can you tell someone*
> *"Let me take the splinter from your eye"*
> *when there's a shingle in your eye?*
>
> *Hypocrite!*
> *First, remove the shingle in your eye*
> *so you can see well enough*
> *to remove the splinter on someone's eye.*
>
> *Don't give dogs what is holy.*
> *Don't give pigs your treasure!*
> *They'd only spit on them*
> *then turn and attack you.*

Pop Choice?
(Mt 7:13–14)

Enter the narrow gate

because
the gate that leads
to destruction is wide
and its highway is spacious.
Many people enter it.

But the gate that leads
to life is small,
and its path is narrow.
Only a few ever find it.

Words and Deeds
(Mt 7:15–20; Lk 6:43–45)

Watch out for religious impostors.
They appear harmless,
but inside, they hunt for victims.

You can identify them by their fruits.
No one picks grapes from thorn bushes
nor figs from thistles.

In the same way,
each tree is known by its fruit.
Good trees produce good fruits,
while bad trees produce bad fruits.
No good tree can produce bad fruit,
nor can a bad tree produce good fruit.

190

*Every tree that does not produce good fruit
is chopped down and thrown to the fire.*

*A good person
brings good things
from the vault of a good heart,
AND
an evil person
brings evil things
from the vault of an evil heart.*

*As such,
your mouth speaks
what your heart contains.*

*So yes, you can identify religious impostors
by their fruits.*

Kingdom of Heaven: Qualifications
(Mt 7:21–23; Lk 6:46)

*Not everyone who calls Me,
"Lord! Lord!"
will enter the Kingdom of Heaven.*

*Only those who do the will
of My Father in heaven.*

*On that day,
many will say to Me,
"Lord! Lord!
Didn't we prophesy in Your Name?
Didn't we exorcise demons in Your Name?
Didn't we perform miracles in Your Name?"*

191

But I will tell them,
"I never knew you.
Get away from Me,
you who commit sins."

So
why call Me "Lord, Lord!"
when you don't do what I say?

Hear + Obey #1
(Mt 7:24–29; Lk 6:47–49, 7:1a)

For sure,
everyone who comes to Me,
hears My words,
AND
applies them
is like a wise person
who digs deep
to lay their house's foundation
on solid rock.

Rain falls, floodwaters rage,
and winds blow to beat on that house,
but it won't collapse nor is it shaken
because it is built well
with its foundation on the rock.

But everyone who hears My words
AND
does not apply them
is like a fool

who builds their house on sand,
without a foundation.

When rain falls, floodwaters rage,
and winds blow to beat on that house,
it immediately falls with an epic crash.

After Jesus finished saying these words, the crowds were amazed at His teaching because He taught authoritatively, unlike the scribes.

The Deeds toward the Big Reveal

Faith = Long Distance Healing #2　　　　　58
(Mt 8:5–13; Lk 7:1b–10)

Time Stamp 　　　　: Rishon/Sunday, 19 August AD 31
Location Stamp 　　: Capernaum, Galilee

Upon the arrival of Jesus, He received a plea from a centurion.

Samlah: 　　　Lord, we come to beg you in behalf of a roman officer whose young servant lies sick at home. His servant is paralysed in terrible pain.

Chanan: 　　　Rabbi, this servant is precious to this officer, so when he heard about You, he sent us to beg You to come and save his servant. His servant is dying, and if anyone deserves Your help, it is him.

Samlah: 　　　He loves our nation and even built a synagogue for us.

Jesus: 　　　*I will come and heal him.*

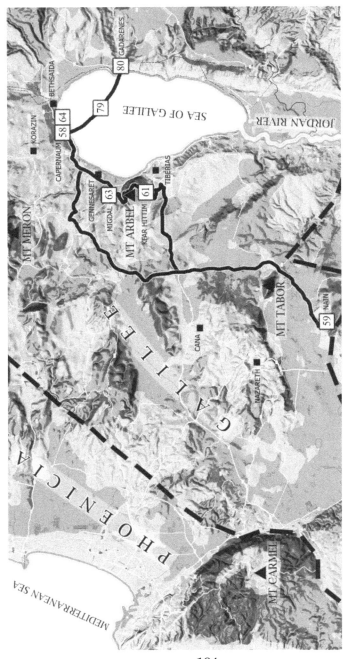

Jesus listened to the people when they interceded for a political enemy. Likewise, He listened to the people after they kicked Him out for exorcising a legion of spiritual enemies.

Jesus went with them but as they approached the officer's house . . .

Herminius: Lord, our friend sent us to give You a message.

Lucretius: He said,

"Lord, don't trouble Yourself.
I am not worthy
to receive You under my roof.
This is why I found myself unworthy
to come to meet You.
Just say a word
and my servant will be healed."

Herminius: He also said,

"I know this because
I too am a man
under the authority
of my superiors and
I too have authority
over my soldiers.

I only need to say
'Go' and they go,
'Come' and they come,
and if I say to my slaves
'Do this,' they do it."

When Jesus heard this, He was amazed at him. He turned to those who followed Him.

Jesus: *I tell you the truth:*
I haven't seen great faith like this
in all of Israel!

I tell you now:
Many will come from all over the world
to sit with Abraham, Isaac, and Jacob
in the Kingdom of Heaven,
but many children from the kingdom
will be thrown outside,
to the darkness,
where there are wails of raging regret.

Jesus then turned to the officer's friends.

Jesus: *Go. Be it as you believed.*

That same hour, the young servant was healed. When everyone sent arrived at the centurion's house, they found the servant healed.

Raising the Dead #1   59
(Lk 7:11–17)

Time Stamp   : Midday, 26 August AD 31
Location Stamp : Nain, Galilee

Jesus went with His disciples to Nain followed by a large crowd. As they approached the village gate, a funeral procession came out. The man who died was a widow's only son. A crowd from the village followed her. When the Lord saw her, He was moved with compassion.

Jesus: *Don't cry.*

He walked to the corpse. The bearers stopped when He touched the bier.

Jesus: *Young man, I tell you, get up.*

The dead sat up and talked! Then Jesus gave him back to his mother.

The crowd was gripped in fear as they praised God.

 Makhela: A Mighty Prophet has risen among us!

 Gerbaal: God has visited His people.

News of Him spread throughout Judea
and the surrounding areas.

Johannes=Elijah=Herald → Messiah=?   60
(Mt 11:1–19; Lk 7:18–35)

Time Stamp   : 2 September AD 31
Location Stamp : Possibly Kafr Hittaya, near Tiberias, Galilee

Jesus went out to teach and preach in towns throughout the region
of Galilee. The disciples of Johannes told him about everything Jesus
did, His teachings, and places where He preached. Since he was in
prison, he sent two of his disciples for an enquiry. When they found
Jesus, they asked Him.

 Kittaw: We are your cousin's disciples. Johannes sent us
                to ask you a question.

 Karoz: Are you the Messiah we've been expecting, or
                should we keep looking for someone else?

At that moment, Jesus had just finished curing many people of their
diseases, illnesses, and evil spirits. He also restored the sight of many
who were blind.

Jesus: *Go back to Johannes and report what you have seen and heard: the blind see, the lame walk, the lepers are cleansed, the deaf hear, the dead are raised to life, and the Good News is being preached to the poor.*

                           Also, blessed are they who do not turn from God because of Me.

As the disciples of Johannes were leaving, Jesus began talking about him to the crowds.

Jesus: *What kind of man*
do you seek in the wilderness —
a reed swayed by the wind,
or a man dressed in fine clothes?
Of course not,
people with expensive clothes
live in palaces.

If you weren't seeking these things,
were you looking for a prophet?

Yes, but Johannes is more than a prophet.
He is the man
the Scriptures refer to
when it says,

"LOOK, I AM SENDING MY MESSENGER AHEAD OF YOU, AND HE WILL PREPARE YOUR WAY BEFORE YOU."

~ Almighty

I tell you the truth:
Of all who were born from women,
not one is greater than Johannes.

Yet even the least person
in the Kingdom of Heaven
is greater than He is!

From the days of Johannes until now,
the Kingdom of Heaven suffers violence,
and violent people are attacking it.

All prophets and the law prophesied
until Johannes came.
And if you are willing to accept it,
he is Elijah, who was prophesied to come.

Everyone with ears, listen!

Everyone who heard this, even the tax collectors, acknowledged God's way as right, for they had been baptised by Johannes. However, the Pharisees and lawyers rejected God's method, for they had refused baptism by Johannes.

Jesus: *To what can I compare this generation?*
            How can I describe them?

            This generation is similar to children playing a game
            in the public square. They complain to their friends,

            "We played wedding songs,
            but you didn't dance,
            so we played funeral songs,
            but you didn't weep."

I say this because
Johannes didn't spend his time
eating and drinking, but you still said,
"He's possessed by a demon."

The Son of Man, on the other hand,
feasts and drinks, then you say,
"He's a glutton, a drunkard,
a friend of tax collectors and of sinners!"

Wisdom, however, is proven right
by those who follow it.

What to do when you see a miracle? 61
(Mt 11:20–24; Lk 10:12–15)

Then Jesus dismissed the cities where He did most of His miracles
because they haven't repented.

Jesus: *Distress awaits you, Korazin & Bethsaida!*

For if My power
was demonstrated in Tyre and Sidon,
they would have sat repenting
in ashes and sackcloth
long long ago.

I tell you,
Tyre and Sidon are better off
on judgement day than you.

Capernaum,
you will not be honoured in heaven.
You will be dragged to Hades.

200

For if the power I demonstrated to you
was made in Sodom,
it would still be here today.

I tell you,
Sodom is better off
on judgement day than you.

Who Anointed Jesus? 62
(Lk 7:36–50)

Time Stamp   : 9 September AD 31
Location Stamp : Possibly Migdal

One of the Pharisees approached Jesus and asked Him to have dinner at his place. Jesus went with him, entered his house, and sat down to eat. A sinful woman heard He was eating in her town so she went and brought an alabaster jar filled with perfume. She stood at His back weeping. She rained her tears on the feet of Jesus and wiped them with her hair. Then she kissed the feet of Jesus with much affection and applied perfume on them.

The Pharisee who invited Jesus saw this, and told himself,

Simon: If this man were a prophet, he would've known who and what kind of woman is touching Him. She's a sinner!

Jesus: *Simon, I have something to tell you.*

Simon: Go ahead, Teacher

Jesus: *A man lent money to two people.*

A King and His Kingdom

One owed him money
worth a salary for 500 days,
the other 50 days.
Both were unable to repay him,
so he kindly cancelled their debts.

Who do you think will love him more?

Simon: I suppose the one who received greater kindness.

Jesus: *Correct judgement!*

He turned to the woman and said to Simon

Jesus: *Do you see this woman?*

When I entered your house,
you didn't offer Me water to wash My feet,
but she wet My feet with her tears
and wiped them with her hair.

You didn't greet Me with a kiss,
while she kept kissing My feet
ever since I got in.

You didn't anoint My head with oil,
but she has anointed My feet with perfume.

Because of her immense love,
I tell you her many sins are forgiven.
But a person who is a bit forgiven
loves just a bit.

To the woman, He said,

Your sins are forgiven.

Those who were at the table started talking.

<u>C</u>heresh:	Forgive? Did He just forgive the woman's sins?
<u>M</u>artinus:	He just did!
<u>C</u>heresh:	He can't do that. Only God can forgive sins.
<u>M</u>artinus:	You are right. Who is He to forgive sins?

Still talking to the woman,

Jesus:	*Your faith has saved you. Go in peace.*

Lessons on the Kingdom of God

The Women in the Entourage of Jesus   63
(Lk 8:1–3)

Time Stamp   : Morning, 16 September AD 31
Location Stamp   : Migdal, Galilee

Soon after, Jesus toured nearby towns and villages, preaching and announcing the Good News about the Kingdom of God. The 12 were with Him, along with some women who had been healed of evil spirits and illnesses. Among them were Mary, a.k.a. Magdalene, who was exorcised of seven demons; Joanna, the wife of Chuza, Herod's house manager; Susanna; and many others who out of their own means attended to the needs of Jesus and His disciples.

Allegation #3: Jesus, Satan, and Parable #2   64
(Mk 3:20–30; Mt 12:22–37; Lk 11:14–28)

Time Stamp   : Midday, 16 September AD 31
Location Stamp   : Capernaum, Galilee

Jesus entered a house and as usual, a crowd gathered with enough size to keep Him and His disciples from eating. Hearing this, those related to Him went out to take Him.

Zebedee:	He's preaching again.
Mary:	But they haven't eaten yet.
Salome:	He could at least rest first so they could eat.
Zebedee:	He's lost it. Come, let's go get Him.

Just then, a demon-possessed man, who was blind and mute, was brought to Jesus. He healed him, and thus, he was able to speak and see. The whole crowd was amazed.

Eleazar:	Could this be the Son of David?
Shammah:	Could He be the Chosen One?
Josheb:	He must be the One we've all been waiting for!

Outside the house where Pharisees and scribes from Jerusalem heard of the miracle said to themselves,

Iose:	You know who can command demons?
Jehumoreh:	Who?

Iose:	Satan, the prince of demons! Who else?
Jehumoreh:	You mean He is Satan in the flesh?
Iose:	No! He gets His authority from Satan. That is how He ejects demons.
Shimeon:	No, He's possessed by Satan! That's how.
Jehumoreh:	He gets His power from Satan?
Psithos:	I heard the experts say the Rabbi gets His power to exorcise from Satan.
Rakhil:	You mean Jesus? Is that how it is?
Nirgan:	Really? Rabbi Jesus commands demons because Satan authorised Him?
Psithos:	That's what the experts said!
Rakhil:	I think one of the scribes said it is because He is possessed by Satan himself.
Alethos:	That can't be right! We better ask Him to prove that He didn't get His authority from Satan.

Some people from the crowd tried to test Jesus, by asking Him to show them a sign from heaven.

Shimeon:	Jesus, if you didn't get your authority from Satan, show us a sign from heaven!
Alethos:	Prove to us you're not in league with the devil!

Iose: Yeah! Show us a sign from heaven!

Knowing what's in their hearts, Jesus called them over and responded in parables.

Jesus: *How can Satan cast out Satan?*
If a kingdom is divided, it can't stand.
It will be destroyed.
If a family or fortress is divided, it can't stand.

Even Satan,
if He contradicts and opposes himself,
he can't stand. His end has come.

If I, who you claim is possessed by Satan,
throw Satan out,
then he is contradicting himself!
How will his kingdom stand?

If I exorcise demons by Satan's authority,
by whose authority
do your pupils exorcise demons?
You're in trouble
once your children hear of this.

However,
if I exorcise demons
by the Spirit of God,
then the Kingdom of God
got you cornered.

You know very well that
no one can break
into a strong man's house to steal

unless He first ties up the strong man.
Only then can the thief ransack his house.

But if that strong man is fully armed,
and guards his mansion,
then he is fully secure.

That is
until Someone stronger overpowers him,
takes away his last line of defence,
then plunders him.

Anyone who is not with Me
is against Me, and
anyone who doesn't gather with Me
will scatter.

Nirgan: It is pointless!
He is possessed
by the prince of demons himself!

Iose: Prove to us you're not possessed
by an evil spirit!

Shimeon: Prove to us you're not possessed by Satan!

Jesus: *I am telling you the truth:*
Whoever speaks a word
against the Son of Man
will be forgiven.

All people's sins
and blasphemy will be forgiven,
however much they blasphemed.

207

A King and His Kingdom

But
whoever blasphemes the Holy Spirit
will never be forgiven,
not in this age, nor in the age to come.
Those people are guilty
of eternal sin.

Make a tree good, and its fruit will be good.
Make a tree bad, and its fruit will be bad.
You know a tree by its fruit.

You generation of vipers!
How could you evil people
say anything good?
Your mouth will say
what is in your heart.

A good person brings good things
from their goods stash,
while an evil person brings evil things
from their evil stash.

I tell you on judgement day
everyone will defend themselves
for every careless word they say.

By your words you will be rendered innocent,
and by your words, you will be condemned.

Loreto:	Happy is the womb that carried You, and happy are the breasts that nursed You!
Jesus:	*Those who hear the word of God and obey are happy indeed.*

The Sign: Dead for a Time   **65**
(Mt 12:38–45; Lk 11:29–32)

The crowd around Jesus was growing when . . .

Iose:
Teacher, we want You to show us a miraculous sign to prove Your authority.

Jesus:
This wicked and adulterous people
demand a sign,
but it will get nothing
except the sign of the prophet Jonah.

Just as Jonah was a sign for the Ninevites,
so will the Son of Man be to these people.

For just as Jonah was inside a great fish
for three days and three nights,
so will the Son of Man be inside earth
for three days and three nights.

On judgement day,
the Ninevites will stand up with these people
and condemn them
because they repented at Jonah's preaching.
But look! Someone greater than Jonah is here.

On judgement day,
the queen of Sheba
will stand up with these people
and condemn them,
for she travelled far
to hear the wisdom of Solomon.

But look!
Someone greater than Solomon is here.

When an impure spirit leaves a person,
it goes through dry places searching.
Not finding rest, it says,
"I will return to the house I left."

Upon arrival,
it finds the house swept clean and in order.
The spirit then finds seven other spirits
more evil than itself,
enters the person, and lives there.
In the end,
the person's condition is worse than ever.

That is how these people are going to be.

Hear + Obey #2: Holy Fam   66
(Mt 12:46–50; Mk 3:31–35; Lk 8:19–21)

Jesus was still speaking to the crowd when His family came. Having a thick crowd around Him, they were unable to reach Him, so they sent someone to call Him.

Chavah: Look! Your mother and Your relatives are standing outside, wanting to see You and talk to You.

Jesus: *Who is My mother and who are My relatives?*

He pointed to His disciples, those seated around Him.

Jesus: *Here are My mother and My relatives,*
          everyone who hears
          the word of God
          and obeys it.
          Yes, all who do
          the will of My Father in heaven
          is My brother, My sister, and My mother!

The Kingdom of God

Introduction
(Mt 8:18a, 13:1–3a; Mk 4:1–2; Lk 8:4)

Time Stamp   : Afternoon, 16 September AD 31
Location Stamp   : shores of Capernaum, Galilee

Later that same day, Jesus left the house and sat beside the sea of Galilee. Soon a large crowd from the city gathered around Him. The crowd was so big that He had to get into a boat where He sat as people stood on the shore.

He taught them many things in parables.

Parable #3: the Sower   67
(Mt 13:3b–9; Mk 4:3–9; Lk 8:5–8)

Jesus: *A farmer went out to sow his seeds. While sowing,*
          some fell along the path where it was trampled and
          devoured by birds of the air. Some seeds fell on rocky
          places where there isn't much soil. The seeds sprouted
          quickly because the soil was shallow and they had no
          moisture. The sun came up, the sprouts were scorched

211

and they withered because they had no root. Other
seeds fell among thorns that grew and choked the seeds
such that it yielded no crop. Still, other seeds fell on
fertile ground where they sprouted, grew, and produced
a crop. One yielded 100, another brought 60, and
still another 30 times the size of what was sown.

Let those who have ears to hear, obey.

Parable #4: The Lamp   68
(Mk 4:21–25; Lk 8:16–18)

Jesus: *Does anyone bring in a lamp*
                  to hide it under the cupboard?
                  or is there anyone
                  who sets their lamp under the bed?

                  No one does that!
                  Instead, they light up the lamp
                  and mount it on a lampstand,
                  so everyone who enters can see the light.

                  Everything concealed is meant to be revealed,
                  and every secret is meant to be exposed.
                  Let those who have ears to hear obey.

                  Pay attention to what you hear.

                  The way you judge
                  is the way you will be judged
                  and more.

Parable #5: The Growing Seed   69
(Mk 4:26–29)

212

Jesus: *The Kingdom of God is like a person who scatters seed on the ground. Night and day, he sleeps and wakes. The seed sprouts and grows, but he never knows how. The earth independently produces a crop. First, the seed grows a stalk, then comes the head that later becomes the grain, which ripens out of sight. When that happens, he takes out his sickle, and swings it because harvest has arrived.*

Parable #6: Wheat and Weeds 70
(Mt 13:24–30)

Jesus: *The Kingdom of Heaven is like a Person who sowed good seed in his field. But the moment everyone slept, the enemy came and sowed weeds among the wheat then escaped. When the seed sprouted and bore grain, the weeds appeared too.*

Workers: *Sir, didn't you sow good seeds in your field?*

Landlord: *Yes*

Workers: *Then where did the weeds come from?*

Landlord: *An enemy. An enemy did this.*

Workers: *Shall we go and pull the weeds out?*

Landlord: *No, if you pull the weeds now, you might uproot the wheat.*

Let both of them grow until harvest. At the right time, I'll instruct harvesters to pull the weeds first,

213

before tying them in bundles to be burned. Afterwards, gather the wheat into my granary.

Parable #7: The Mustard Seed   71
(Mk 4:30–32; Lk 13:18–19; Mt 13:31–32)

Jesus: *What is the Kingdom of God like?*
To what can we compare it?
With what parable shall we illustrate it?

The Kingdom of Heaven is like a mustard seed that a farmer sowed in his field. Even though it is the smallest of all seeds that were sown, it becomes the largest among garden plants, grows into a tree with huge branches where birds come and nest.

Parable #8: The Yeast   72
(Mt 13:33; Lk 13:20–21)

Jesus: *What else is the Kingdom of God like?*

The Kingdom of Heaven is like the yeast a woman used in making bread. Even though she put only a little yeast in 33 quarts of flour, it permeated every part of the dough until it was entirely leavened.

Parable of the Sower Explained   73
(Mt 13:36a, 10–23; Mk 4:10–20, 36a; Lk 8:9–15)

Time Stamp   : Late afternoon, 16 September AD 31

Still at the shores of the sea of Galilee, Jesus dismissed the crowds and went indoor. As soon as Jesus was alone, His 12 disciples and women who supported Him came.

Simon (Peter): Why do You use parables when You talk to the people?

Jesus: *The knowledge of the mysteries of the Kingdom of God has been given to you, but not to them.*

Whoever has knowledge
of the Kingdom of God,
will be given more
such that they'll have an abundance.
Those who have no knowledge
of the Kingdom of God,
even what they have will be taken away.

When I speak to outsiders in parables,
the prophecy of Isaiah is fulfilled:

"EVEN THOUGH THEY LOOK, THEY CAN'T SEE OR PERCEIVE. EVEN THOUGH THEY LISTEN, THEY COULD NEITHER HEAR NOR UNDERSTAND."

~ God Almighty

It is because these people's hearts
have grown cold.
Their ears have dulled,
and they have closed their eyes.

But if they see with their eyes,
hear with their ears,
understand with their hearts and turn,
I would heal and forgive them.

But blessed are your eyes
because they see
and your ears
because they hear.

I tell you the truth:
Many prophets and righteous people
longed to see what you see but didn't and
longed to hear what you hear but didn't.

Barsabbas: What does the parable of the sower mean?

Jesus: *If you don't understand this parable,*
then how will you understand
the other parables?

Listen closely to the parable of the sower.
This is what it means:

The farmer sows the word of God, which is the seed.
Some ears are like the seeds along the path, where the
word is sown. When people hear the word of the
kingdom but fail to understand, Satan comes and
robs the word that was sown in their heart to keep
them from believing and to keep them from being
saved.

Others are like the seeds sown on rocky places. They
hear the word of God and immediately receive it with
joy. But since they have no root, they believe only for
a moment. When trouble or persecution comes because
of the word, they quickly fall into sin.

Then there are others who are similar to seeds sown
among thorns. They hear God's word, but as they live

216

their life, the word is choked by the worries of the world, the delusion of abundance, and the pleasure from their desires. These things choke the word resulting to nothing.

Yet others are like seeds sown on fertile ground. They are those who have good and virtuous hearts. They hear the word of God, receive it, understand it, cling to it, and by persevering, they produce results that are 30, 60, or even a 100 times the amount planted!

Comment on Jesus' use of Parables   74
(Mk 4:33–34; Mt 13:34–35)

Jesus taught the word to people with many similar parables that they are able to understand. Everything He taught the people came in parables. But when He's alone with His disciples, He explained everything to them.

This fulfilled the prophet's message:

**"*I WILL SPEAK TO YOU IN PARABLES.*
I WILL EXPLAIN THINGS HIDDEN
SINCE THE CREATION OF THE WORLD."**

~ God Almighty

Parable of the Wheat and Weeds Explained   75
(Mt 13:36b–43)

Simon (Peter):   Explain to us the parable of the weeds in the field.

217

Jesus: *I am the farmer who plants the good seed. The field is the world, and the good seeds are the children of the Kingdom. The weeds are the evil one's children and the enemy who sows them is the devil. The harvest is the end of the age, and the harvesters are the angels.*

At the end of the age, it will be similar to the way weeds are pulled out and burned. The Son of Man will send His angels to weed the Kingdom out of everything that causes sin and everyone who commits sin. The angels will then throw them into the blazing furnace, where beings weep and gnash their teeth. Then the righteous will shine like the sun in their Father's Kingdom.

Anyone who has ears to hear, must obey!

Parable #9: The Hidden Treasure   76
(Mt 13:44)

The Kingdom of Heaven is like treasure hidden in a field. Someone found the treasure and hid it again. With much joy, the person sold everything he owned then purchased that field.

Parable #10: The Pearl Merchant   77
(Mt 13:45–46)

Again, the Kingdom of Heaven is like a merchant searching for fine pearls. The moment the merchant found that one pearl with great value, he went away to sell everything he owned and bought it!

Parable #11: The Fishing Net 78
(Mt 13:47–53, 8:18b–20; Mk 4:35)

> *Again, the Kingdom of Heaven is like a fishing net cast into the sea and caught all kinds of fish. When the net was full, it was pulled ashore. People sat down, and sorted good fish into containers but threw the bad away.*
>
> *That is how it will be at the end of age. Angels will come and separate the wicked from the righteous. Then they'll throw the wicked into the blazing furnace, where beings weep and gnash their teeth.*
>
> *Do you understand all these things?*

Simon (Peter): Yes, we do.

Jesus: *In understanding these parables, every scribe who is taught in the Kingdom of Heaven is like a homeowner who brings new and old treasures from their vault.*

Time Stamp : Evening, 16 September AD 31

After telling these parables, Jesus gave His disciples instructions.

Jesus: *Let's cross the lake to the other side.*

King of the Kingdom: Signs and Feats

Feat #1: God over Nature 79
(Mk 4:36b–41; Mt 8:23–27; Lk 8:22–25)

---

*"God calms the storm
and stills its waves"*

- Psalms 107:29

Time Stamp   : Evening, 16 September AD 31
Location Stamp   : Sea of Galilee

Jesus got on one boat with the disciples left. Other boats followed. While sailing, Jesus fell asleep and a violent whirlwind blew on the lake. The waves were breaking onto the boat, filling it with water, endangering their lives.

The disciples went to the back of the boat where Jesus slept with His head on a cushion.

Simon (Peter): Master! Master, we're dying!

Nathanael: Lord, save us!

John: Teacher, don't You care if we die?

Jesus woke up.

Jesus: *Oligopistos! Why are you so afraid?*

Jesus rebuked the wind and it died. To the raging waves, He said,

Jesus: *Silence!*

. . . And commanded,

Jesus: *Be still!*

. . . The raging waters stopped, and there was a great calm.

Jesus:	*Why are you so afraid?*
	Where is your faith?
	Don't you have faith yet?

The disciples were amazed, in awe, and terrified at the same time.

Judas:	Who is this Man?
Barsabbas:	What kind of Man is He?
Matthias:	He commands wind and water, and they obey Him!
Stephen:	Even the sea obeys Him!

Feat #2: Ultimate Exorcist   80
(Mk 5:1–20; Mt 8:28–34; Lk 8:26–39)

Time Stamp   : Morning, 17 September AD 31
Location Stamp : Gergesa (Kursi), Region of Gadarenes

They arrived on the other side of the sea of Galilee, in the region of Gadarenes, where the Gerasenes lived. As Jesus stepped out of the boat, two demon-possessed men from the tombs saw Him and ran out of town to meet Him.

One of them was possessed by many demons. These demons often took control of the man and drove him to lonely places. Naked and homeless, he stayed in the cemetery and could not be tied up, even with chains. He had been chained with shackles many times in the past, but he only broke the chains and shattered the shackles. Now, no one was strong enough to subdue him. Day and night, in tombs and hills, he would shriek and cut himself with stones. He was so violent that no one dares to go through the cemetery.

Jesus: *Come out of the man!*

One of them was exorcised, but the other one shrieked and bowed low before Him shouting out,

A̲zazel: What do you want with me, Jesus, Son of God Most High? Did You come to torture us before the appointed time? I beg You, in the name of God, don't torture me!

Jesus: *What is your name?*

Legion: My name is Legion,
                   because there are many of us in him.
                   Please do not exile me.
                   Do not send me away please.
                   Do not banish us to the bottomless pit.
                   Let us stay here.
                   Please do not kick us out of the country.
                   Do not banish us from this place.
                   Do not send me to the abyss

There was a large herd of pigs feeding on the nearby hillside.

Legion: We beg You, if you cast us out, send us to those pigs. Please send us to that herd, so we may enter them.

Jesus: *Go!*

Jesus gave them permission. The demons came out of the man, entered the herd. All 2,000 pigs rushed down the steep bank and drowned in the sea. Those who fed the pigs ran and reported what happened to the town. These same witnesses would later spread the story to the surrounding countryside.

Everyone in town rushed out as soon as they heard the story. When they saw the dead pigs, they went to Jesus and found the man possessed by the legion of demons sitting there, sane and fully clothed. Those who saw the exorcism told the townsfolk about the pigs and how the demon-possessed man had been healed. Out of great fear, the Gerasenes begged Jesus to leave their region.

As Jesus was boarding,

Azazel: If You may, please let me come with You.

Jesus: *Go home. Tell them how the Lord had mercy on you and everything He has done for you.*

Azazel obeyed and went to the Decapolis, sharing everything Jesus did for him, and everyone was amazed. Jesus took the boat and headed back.

Feat #3: No Look + Raising the Dead #2   81
(Mt 9:18–26; Mk 5:21–43; Lk 8:40–56)

"power came out from Him healing"

~ Luke

Time Stamp   : Later that same day, 17 September AD 31
Location Stamp : Gennesaret, Galilee

Back to the other side of the lake, a large crowd who had been waiting for Jesus gathered around Him at the shore. Jairus, a leader of the local synagogue, arrived. The moment he saw Jesus, he knelt at His feet, begging.

Jairus: My only daughter is dying. Please come to my
               house, lay Your hands on her, and heal her so she
               can live.

Jesus got up and went with him along with His disciples. The
daughter of Jairus is 12 years old. The people followed, crowding
around Him. A woman who heard about Jesus came with the crowd.

Veronica: If I can touch His tallit, I will be healed.

Following Him from behind, she touched His tallit's tzitzit. The
bleeding immediately stopped, and she felt that her body has been
healed of its affliction. Jesus felt healing power come out of Him, so
He turned to the crowd.

Jesus: *Who touched My clothes?*

People around Him denied touching Him.

Simon (Peter): You know this crowd around you
               is pressing on You.
               How can You ask, "Who touched Me?"

Jesus: *I know someone touched Me*
               because I felt power come out from Me.

Knowing she couldn't hide what happened to her, the frightened
woman came forward trembling, fell in front of Him and told Him
the truth.

Veronica: It was me. I needed healing. I have been bleeding
               for 12 years and travelled to find the best
               physicians I can find, but none of them was able
               to cure me. Some of their treatments even made

224

it worse. I have exhausted all that I have, and I have nowhere to go. So when I heard about You, I thought that if I can touch the tip of Your garment, You will heal me. So, when I touched You, I . . . I . . . I felt my bleeding stopped. I . . . I . . . don't know what happened and then You started asking, so . . .

Jesus: *Daughter, take courage,*
              your faith has healed you.

Veronica: I have nothing to pay you. I live in isolation, unclean, and my affliction have caused you this inconvenience. I . . .

Jesus: *Go in peace,*
              you have been made whole
              from your affliction.

As He spoke to her, people from the house of Jairus came and spoke to him privately.

Arik: Your daughter is dead. It's pointless to trouble the Teacher now. Let's head home.

Jesus: *Fear not. Believe and she will be healed.*

Upon entering the official's home, He heard the flute playing and saw the troubled crowd mourning with much wailing.

Jesus: *Get out! What's with all this commotion? Why are you weeping? The child isn't dead. She's only sleeping.*

225

The crowd laughed at Him because they all knew she's dead. He sent the people out and didn't let anyone in. He also kept the people following Him from entering, all except Peter, John, James, and the child's parents.

After the crowd was sent out, they entered the room where the girl lay. Jesus held her hand.

Jesus: *Talitha koum (Little girl, arise!)*

The girl got up with a gasp and started walking. They were overwhelmed with ecstasy. Jesus ordered them to give her something to eat and gave strict instructions not to tell anyone what happened, and yet the report spread throughout the land.

Feat #4: Heal Two and Two-in-One 82
(Mt 9:27–34)

Jesus left the house of Jairus and travelled back to Capernaum.

Time Stamp   : Afternoon, 17 September AD 31
Location Stamp   : Capernaum, Galilee

Approaching His house, two blind people followed shouting,

Eleazar: Son of David!

Shammah: Have mercy on us!

Jesus was already inside the house when they finally caught up.

Jesus: *Do you believe I can do this?*

Both: Yes, Lord.

He touched their eyes.

Jesus: *Be it so, according to your faith.*

Their eyes were opened. Jesus then gave them strict instructions.

Jesus: *No one should know about this.*

However, they went out and made Him famous all over the region.

Time Stamp   : 18 September AD 31

Next day, as Jesus and His disciples were leaving, people brought a mute who is demon-possessed. After exorcising the demon, the mute began to speak. The crowds were amazed.

Aspasia: This has never been seen anywhere in Israel!

Qarob-nāḥāš: It is by the power of the prince of demons that He exorcise demons.

Ambassadors of the Kingdom of God

Rejected at Nazareth #2   83
(Mk 6:1–6a; Mt 13:54–58; Jn 4:44)

Jesus left Capernaum followed by His disciples and went to Nazareth, where He was raised.

Time Stamp   : Sabbath, 22 September AD 31
Location Stamp   : Nazareth, Galilee

When Sabbath came, He began teaching in the synagogue, and many who heard Him were astonished while others took pot shots at Him.

Eudocia:	Where did He get these ideas?
Doronia:	What marvellous wisdom God gave Him!
Eudocia:	I heard that He did so many miracles in Capernaum!
Doronia:	Where did He get that power? Isn't He a carpenter?
Datan:	Yeah, the Son of carpenter. Isn't His mother named Mary?
Korach:	He's a relative of James, Joseph, Judas, and Simon.
Abeiron:	His aunts live here among us too.
Eudocia:	Then where did He get all these?
Jesus:	*A prophet is never honoured in their hometown, among relatives, not even their own household.*

Because of their lack of faith, He was unable to do much mighty work other than to lay His hands on a few sick people and heal. Amazed at their unbelief, He went around teaching in other villages.

Wanted: Workers   84
(Mk 6:6b; Mt 9:35–38)

Time Stamp   : 28 September AD 31
Location Stamp   : Jerusalem, Judea
Indicative Event : Arrival in Jerusalem in preparation for Feast of Trumpets

Time Stamp   : 27 October AD 31
Location Stamp   : Jerusalem Judea
Indicative Event : Last day in Jerusalem
                   to celebrate Shmini Atzeret/Simchat Torah

Time Stamp   : 30 October AD 31
Location Stamp   : Somewhere in Galilee

Jesus travelled through all the towns and villages, teaching in their synagogues, announcing the Good News about the Kingdom, while healing every kind of disease and illness. Watching the crowds, He was moved with compassion for them because they were weary and disheartened, like sheep without a shepherd.

Time Stamp   : 19 December AD 31
Location Stamp   : Somewhere in Galilee
Indicative Event : Departure from Galilee

Jesus:

The harvest is great,
but the workers are few.
So then,
seek the Lord of the harvest
and ask Him to send
more workers to His field.

Time Stamp   : 21 December AD 31
Location Stamp   : Jerusalem, Judea
Indicative Event : Arrival in Jerusalem in preparation for Hanukkah.
                   Around Jesus' birthday.

Despite the increasing greatness of Jesus' deeds,
He still expressed the need for more harvesters.

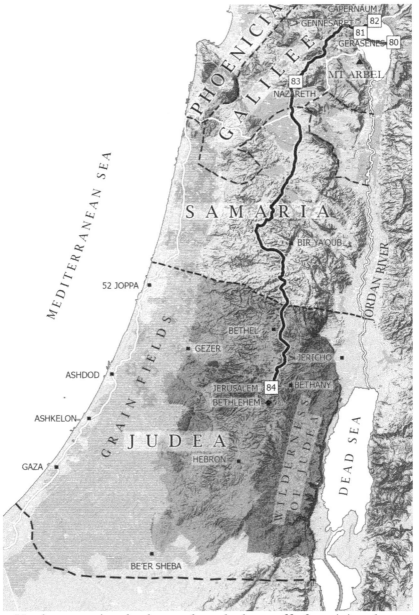

He then appoints leaders and sends them off after giving them
authority and power like no prophet ever did before.

MARK

1	2	3	4
5	6	7	8
9	10	11	12
13	14	15	16

JOHN

1	2	3	4	5	6	7
8	9	10	11	12	13	14
15	16	17	18	19	20	21

MATTHEW

1	2	3	4	5	6	7
8	9	10	11	12	13	14
15	16	17	18	19	20	21
22	23	24	25	26	27	28

LUKE

1	2	3	4	5	6
7	8	9	10	11	12
13	14	15	16	17	18
19	20	21	22	23	24

A chart showing all chapters of each Gospel. The shading indicates the progress of the narrative with respect to each chapter and book. A shading of John's title block means 25% has been covered. Trivia: 33% of the 4 Gospels have been covered at the end of this book.

ACKNOWLEDGEMENTS

Almighty – for life, for His patience, for His healing, for His guidance, for His pardon, for all that I have, for all that I am.

My parents – who have set a benchmark on how to serve the Almighty with all that you have and all that you are. Your life is the standard I try to live by.

My siblings – whose presence in my life is a reminder that I am myself and that I'll always have friends and playmates all my life.

My children – who remind me to stay faithful, playful, child-like, gentle, loving, responsible, and be more than I am. I pray that your interest in knowing God may be sparked either by this book or the Bible itself. May you fall in love to Him who is ever reliable and ever faithful.

My love, my life, my person – Charissa – who healed my doubt in God's will and His forgiveness, and in making His love concrete in my life, in her, in us both, and our family.

Everyone who was there when I was undergoing treatment for cancer and everyone who prayed for me, this book is out because of the charity you have shown me. You made the hand and face of God real in my life.

Everyone who funded this book because I didn't have enough in hand to get this published, thank you all so much.

To everyone I have encountered and walked with in my life, you all have varying degrees of impact to my life. This book is shaped by that time I spent with you all.